Mary:
May all your
Troubles FLY
away in the new
year and peace
abide with
you this season
LOVE.
JOAN

1001

PATCHWORK

DESIGNS

MAGGIE MALONE

 Sterling Publishing Co., Inc.   New York

ACKNOWLEDGMENTS

I would like to thank my daughter, Kelly, for the many hours she spent helping me prepare this book. Without her assistance I could never have completed the manuscript on time.

And a thank you to my mother, Ann DeWeese, for her patience in putting up with papers and books sprawling all over her house.

Library of Congress Cataloging in Publication Data

Malone, Maggie, 1942–
    1001 patchwork designs.

    Bibliography: p.
    Includes indexes.
    1. Patchwork—Patterns.   I. Title.
II. Title: One thousand one patchwork designs.
III. Title: One thousand and one patchwork
designs.
TT835.M347   746.46′041   81-85037
ISBN 0-8069-5460-4   AACR2
ISBN 0-8069-5461-2 (lib. bdg.)
ISBN 0-8069-7604-7 (pbk.)

Copyright © 1982 by Sterling Publishing Co., Inc.
Two Park Avenue, New York, N.Y. 10016
Distributed in Australia by Oak Tree Press Co., Ltd.
P.O. Box K514 Haymarket, Sydney 2000, N.S.W.
Distributed in the United Kingdom by Blandford Press
Link House, West Street, Poole, Dorset BH15 1LL, England
Distributed in Canada by Oak Tree Press Ltd.
% Canadian Manda Group, 215 Lakeshore Boulevard East
Toronto, Ontario M5A 3W9
Manufactured in the United States of America

Contents

Introduction

Quiltmaking's continued popularity attests to its ability to offer something for everyone. Perhaps you made a quilt for the warmth and charm it gives a room. Or for the opportunity it gives you to put your own personal stamp on your surroundings. Or the satisfaction derived when you present a quilt to someone special, made to suit their tastes and decor. It's a wonderful creative outlet for experiments in color and design. It may be your form of tranquillizer, soothing away the day's tensions with each stitch you take. Or you may enjoy the challenge of competition, testing your design ability and workmanship against all other entrants.

Every stage of making a quilt has something to offer. Perhaps you like the planning stage, choosing just the right colors and tracking down the fabrics. Or the piecing, watching the colors interact and bringing the design alive beneath your fingers. Or perhaps you prefer the quilting stage, taking the tiny, perfect stitches needed to make a masterpiece quilt.

For whatever reason you make a quilt, there are shortcuts and speed techniques to get you over the drudgery to the part you really love to do. To the purists a quilt is a quilt only when made from 100% cotton, with every stitch taken by hand, and the quilting stitches 20 to the inch. I've often marvelled at the beauty and intricacy of the quilts created by hand —and at the patience required to execute them.

However, not every quilt is intended to be a masterpiece. And some of us don't sew very well by hand, and really don't want to take the time to learn, especially when we have our speedy little sewing machines to do the work for us. A quilt made on the sewing machine can be just as beautiful as those done by hand.

In my classes I try to give my students a thorough grounding in the basics, then I encourage them to experiment. I don't lay down hard and fast dos and don'ts. The correct method is whatever method works for you to achieve results of which you can be proud. I believe in simplifying. Quiltmaking is a simple craft, but as with every other craft, there are those who attempt to imbue it with mystery and obscurity, which does nothing but frighten the beginner, for one can never hope to achieve the artificial standards set up by those in the "inner circle."

This book contains 1,001 patterns, but it is by no means all-inclusive. For the most part, I've tried to stick with the simple geometric designs that are easy to draw up, but there are more difficult patterns for the experienced quilter. The designs are grouped according to the number of patches, making up the block, such as 4-patch, 9-patch, and so on. Each one is clearly marked with graph lines to enable you to scale the block to any size desired. An additional benefit is that as you work with the patterns in this book you will learn to recognize the underlying construction of any block you see.

You will also note that within each group many of the pattern pieces are interchangeable. For instance, if you draft a pattern for a 9-patch block, you can also make Patience 9-patch and Red Cross with those same pattern pieces. When you draft the Hourglass pattern, you can also make Calico Puzzle, Shoofly, Snowball, Friendship Star, Box, and several others, by using the same pattern pieces.

The sections on pattern drafting explain how to scale a block to any size. Whether you work by hand or with the sewing machine, there are techniques that can be of use to you in achieving smooth, perfectly aligned blocks.

With the methods given here you can adapt and combine patterns to create truly unique quilts.

METRIC EQUIVALENCY CHART

CONVERTING INCHES TO CENTIMETRES AND YARDS TO METRES

mm — millimetres   cm — centimetres   m — metres

INCHES INTO MILLIMETRES AND CENTIMETRES
(SLIGHTLY ROUNDED FOR YOUR CONVENIENCE)

inches	mm		cm	inches	cm	inches	cm
1/8	3mm			7	18	29	73.5
1/4	6mm			8	20.5	30	76
3/8	10mm	or	1cm	9	23	31	78.5
1/2	13mm	or	1.3cm	10	25.5	32	81.5
5/8	15mm	or	1.5cm	11	28	33	84
3/4	20mm	or	2cm	12	30.5	34	86.5
7/8	22mm	or	2.2cm	13	33	35	89
1	25mm	or	2.5cm	14	35.5	36	91.5
1 1/4	32mm	or	3.2cm	15	38	37	94
1 1/2	38mm	or	3.8cm	16	40.5	38	96.5
1 3/4	45mm	or	4.5cm	17	43	39	99
2	50mm	or	5cm	18	46	40	102
2 1/2	65mm	or	6.3cm	19	48.5	41	104
3	75mm	or	7.5cm	20	51	42	107
3 1/2	90mm	or	9cm	21	53.5	43	109
4	100mm	or	10cm	22	56	44	112
4 1/2	115mm	or	11.5cm	23	58.5	45	115
5	125mm	or	12.5cm	24	61	46	117
5 1/2	140mm	or	14cm	25	63.5	47	120
6	150mm	or	15cm	26	66	48	122
				27	68.5	49	125
				28	71	50	127

YARDS TO METRES
(SLIGHTLY ROUNDED FOR YOUR CONVENIENCE)

YARDS	METRES	YARDS	METRES	YARDS	METRES	YARDS	METRES	YARDS	METRES
1/8	0.15	2 1/8	1.95	4 1/8	3.80	6 1/8	5.60	8 1/8	7.45
1/4	0.25	2 1/4	2.10	4 1/4	3.90	6 1/4	5.75	8 1/4	7.55
3/8	0.35	2 3/8	2.20	4 3/8	4.00	6 3/8	5.85	8 3/8	7.70
1/2	0.50	2 1/2	2.30	4 1/2	4.15	6 1/2	5.95	8 1/2	7.80
5/8	0.60	2 5/8	2.40	4 5/8	4.25	6 5/8	6.10	8 5/8	7.90
3/4	0.70	2 3/4	2.55	4 3/4	4.35	6 3/4	6.20	8 3/4	8.00
7/8	0.80	2 7/8	2.65	4 7/8	4.50	6 7/8	6.30	8 7/8	8.15
1	0.95	3	2.75	5	4.60	7	6.40	9	8.25
1 1/8	1.05	3 1/8	2.90	5 1/8	4.70	7 1/8	6.55	9 1/8	8.35
1 1/4	1.15	3 1/4	3.00	5 1/4	4.80	7 1/4	6.65	9 1/4	8.50
1 3/8	1.30	3 3/8	3.10	5 3/8	4.95	7 3/8	6.75	9 3/8	8.60
1 1/2	1.40	3 1/2	3.20	5 1/2	5.05	7 1/2	6.90	9 1/2	8.70
1 5/8	1.50	3 5/8	3.35	5 5/8	5.15	7 5/8	7.00	9 5/8	8.80
1 3/4	1.60	3 3/4	3.45	5 3/4	5.30	7 3/4	7.10	9 3/4	8.95
1 7/8	1.75	3 7/8	3.55	5 7/8	5.40	7 7/8	7.20	9 7/8	9.05
2	1.85	4	3.70	6	5.50	8	7.35	10	9.15

Creating
With Color

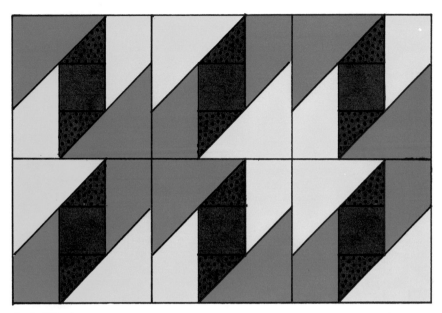

Attic Window

Two ways to use color for a completely different quilt.

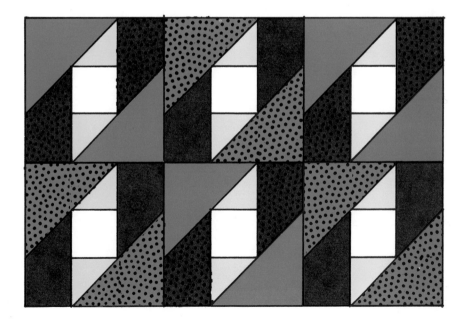

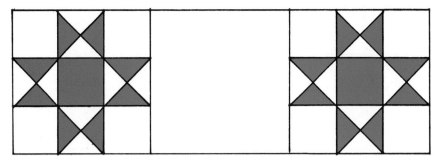

Set with alternate plain blocks.

Diagonal set gives the Ohio Star pattern a new look. Lattice strips could also be used between the blocks.

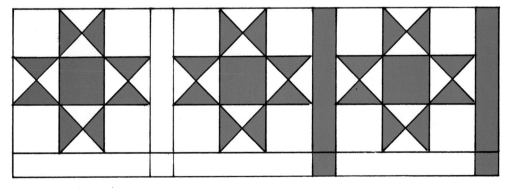

Set with lattice strips.

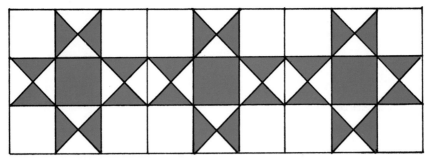

Blocks set solid.

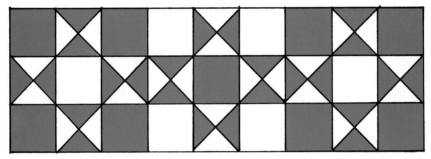

Pattern becomes a form of Shoofly when dark and light colors are alternated from block to block.

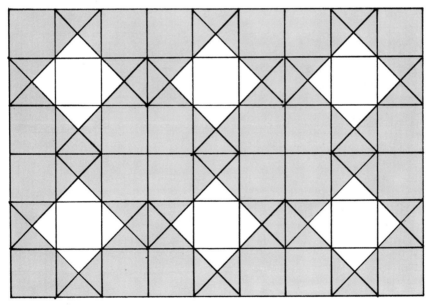

Ohio Star pattern—the color sequence has been changed so that a whole new pattern emerges.

Windblown Square

Set with alternate plain blocks, the design creates an
entirely different quilt than when set solid.

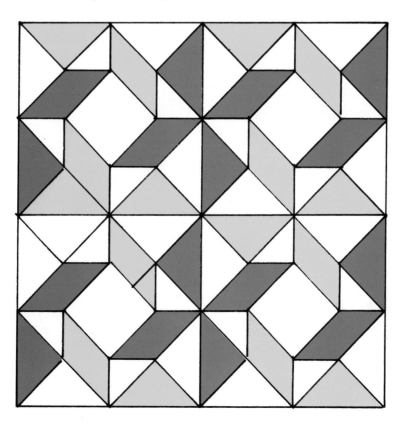

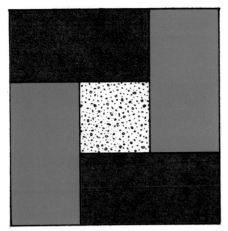

Twist

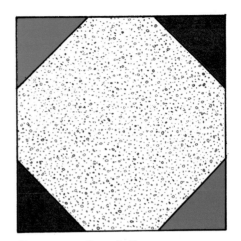

Octagon or Snowball

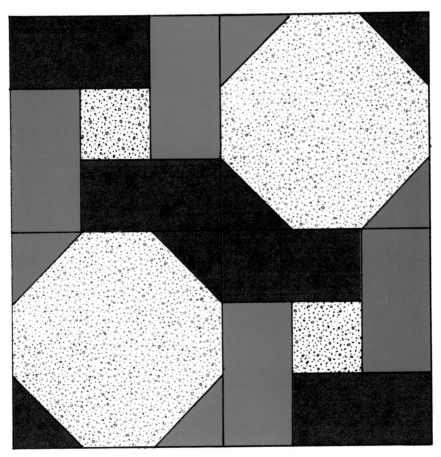

Snowball and Twist become Caning.

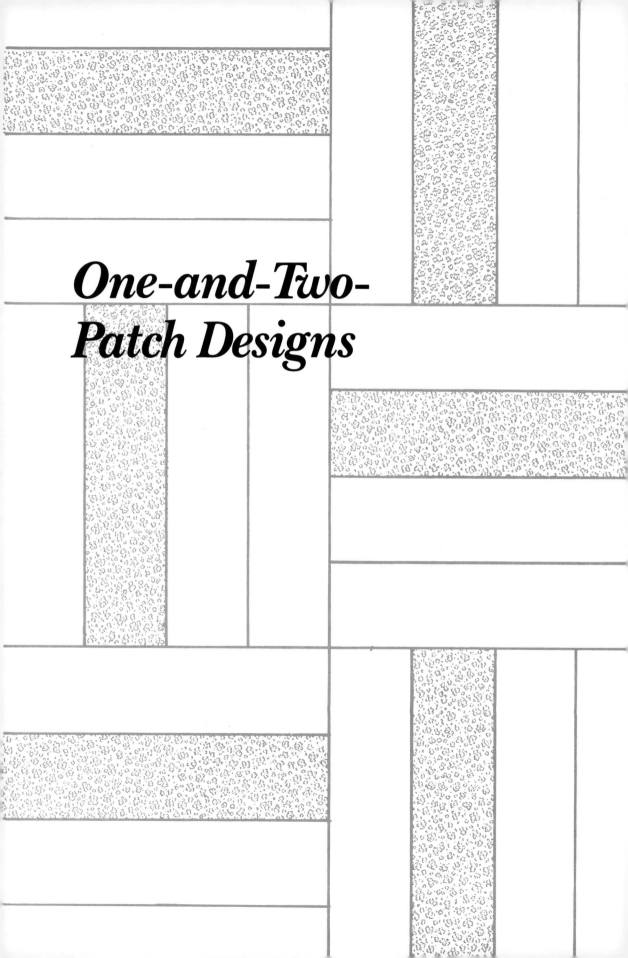

One-and-Two- Patch Designs

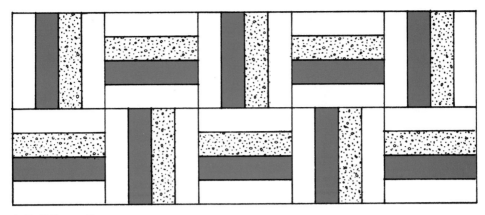

1 Rail Fence I

2 Rail Fence II, each of the color triangles is a different color.

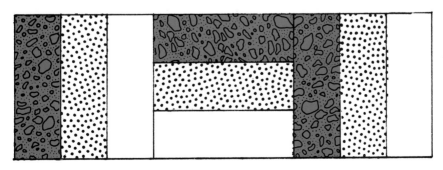

3 Basket Weave

4 London Stairs I

7 Wild Goose Chase I

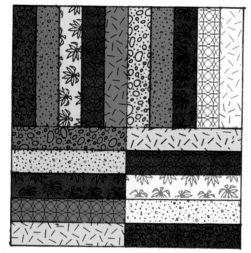

5 Country Charm

6 Tumbler

8 Tree Everlasting I

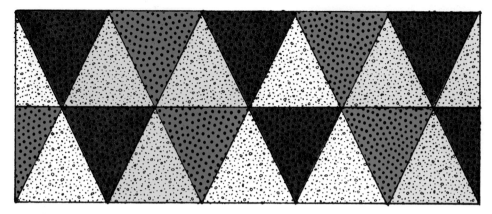

9 Triangles I

10 Honeycomb

11 Spools

12 Clamshell

13 Thousand Pyramids

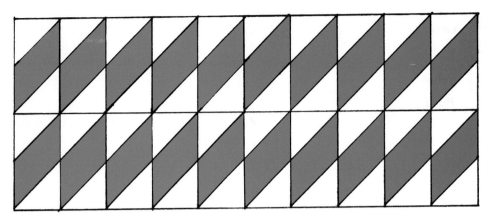

14 Streak of Lightning I

15 Brick

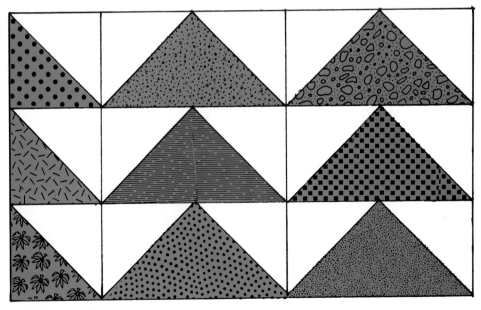

16 Triangles II

17 Diamond Flower Basket

18 Land of Pharaoh

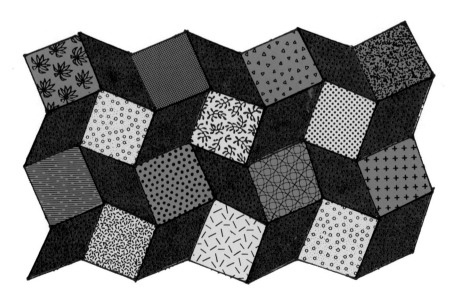

19 Magic Squares

20 Rail Fence III

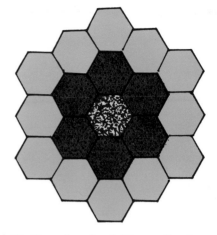

21 Grandmother's Flower Garden

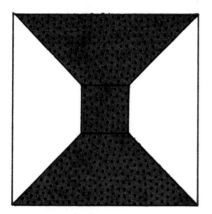

22 Spools II

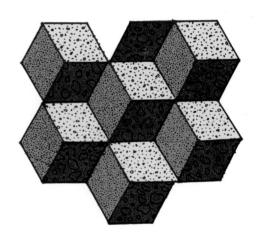

24 Baby Blocks

23 Honeycomb II

21

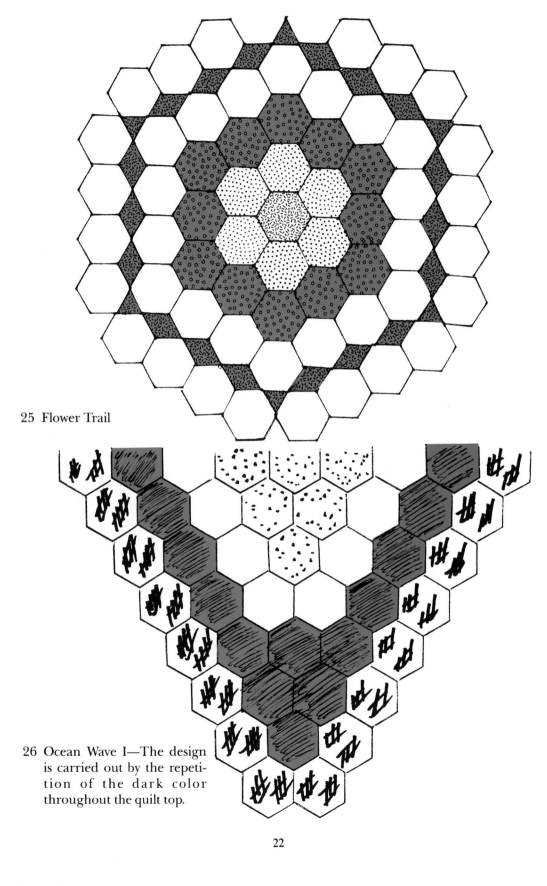

25 Flower Trail

26 Ocean Wave I—The design is carried out by the repetition of the dark color throughout the quilt top.

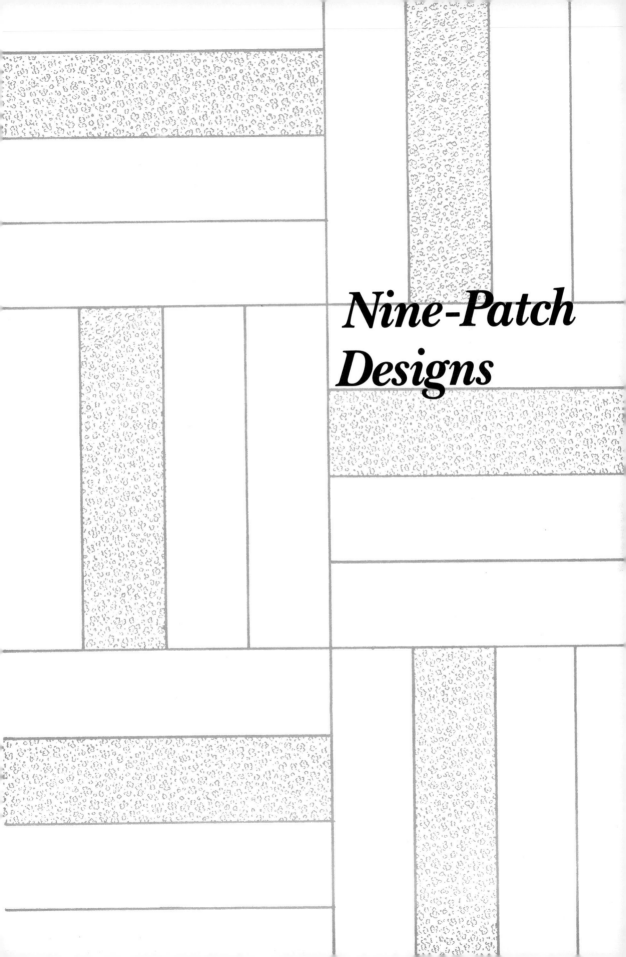

Nine-Patch Designs

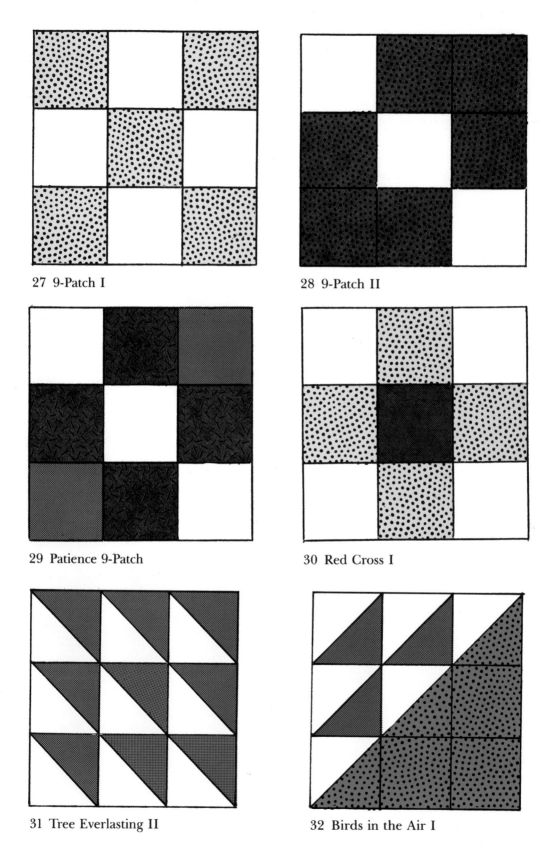

27 9-Patch I

28 9-Patch II

29 Patience 9-Patch

30 Red Cross I

31 Tree Everlasting II

32 Birds in the Air I

The major advantage of being able to draft a pattern is the flexibility it allows you in designing a quilt. For a sampler quilt, you can scale all the blocks to the same size. You might want to make a large medallion type of quilt, and with a little knowledge of pattern construction, it's a simple matter to draft the pattern up in size.

Another advantage is that you know it's accurate. Most printed patterns are off slightly, with the result that the finished pieces will not fit together properly. This is usually caused by distortion in the printing process, but there are honest mistakes made, too.

If you are using the patterns in this book you will note that most of them have graph lines underlying the design areas. This allows you to see how many squares make up each block, and the divisions within each square.

At this point you should decide how large to make the finished block. I don't like working with fractions, so I always try to scale the block in even numbers. For example, a 9-patch block would be drawn with each square equalling 3″ or 4″, giving a finished block of 9″ or 12″. But if I were to make this an 8″ block, I'd be dealing with fractions throughout.

Now to muddy the waters a bit. In drafting patterns I've found that a basic 9-patch can be further broken down by dividing each square in half or into thirds, and in some instances into fourths. In these cases, you can't figure final block size from the basic 9-patch, but must deal with the total number of squares in the block.

The following diagrams illustrate each pattern type and how to arrive at a final block size.

Basic 9-Patch

Square = Final Block Size

1″ = 3″ block
2″ = 6″ block
3″ = 9″ block
4″ = 12″ block
5″ = 15″ block
6″ = 18″ block

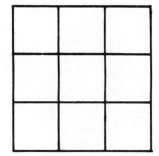

33 Hourglass I

34 Calico Puzzle

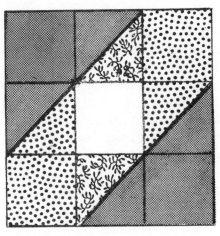

35 Attic Window

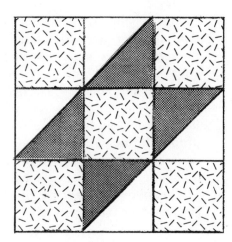

36 Contrary Wife I

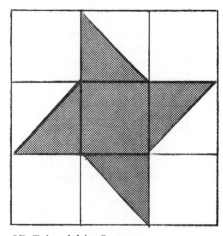

37 Friendship Star

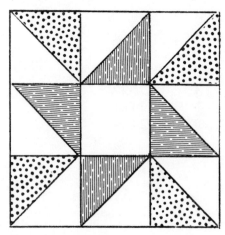

38 9-Patch Star I

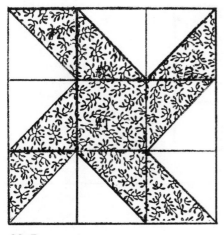

39 Box

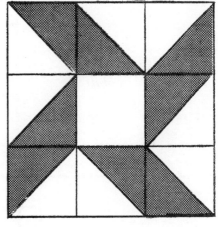

40 Formal Garden I

41 Snowball I

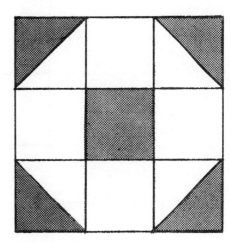

42 Snowball Variation

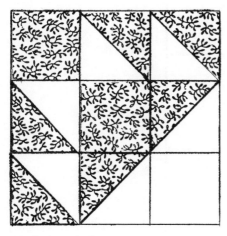

43 Sawtooth I

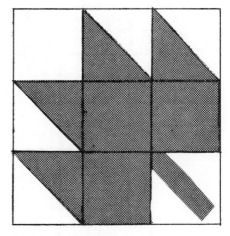

44 Maple Leaf I

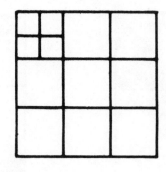

9-Patch
Divided in Half

1″ = 6″ block
2″ = 12″ block
3″ = 15″ block
4″ = 24″ block

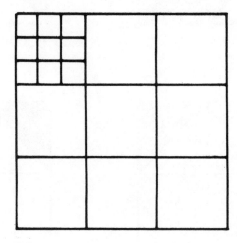

9-Patch
Divided into Thirds

1″ = 9″ block
2″ = 18″ block

9-Patch Divided into Fourths

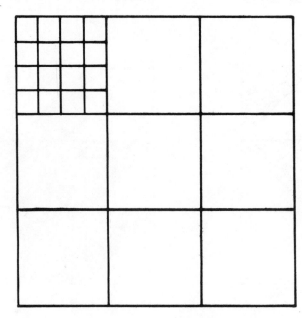

1″ = 12″ block
2″ = 24″ block

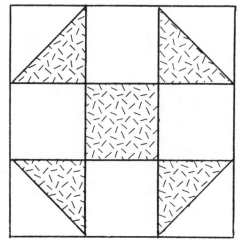

45 Shoofly I

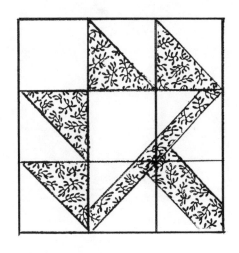

46 Cactus Bud

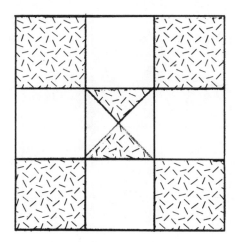

47 Practical Orchard

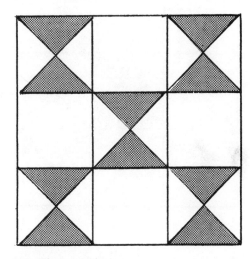

48 Clown's Choice

49 Malvina's Chain

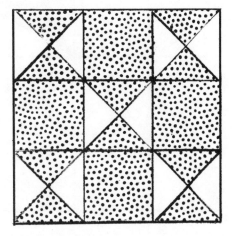

50 Letter-X I

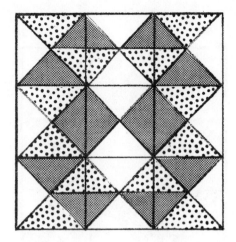

51 Buckwheat

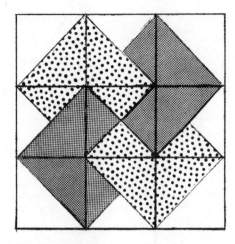

52 Card Tricks

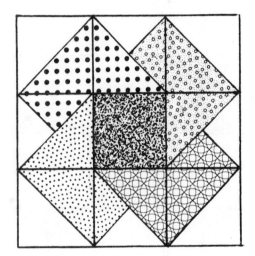

53 Color Wheel

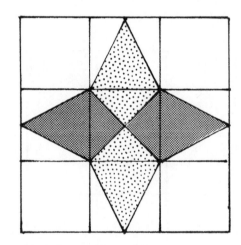

54 Arkansas Snowflake

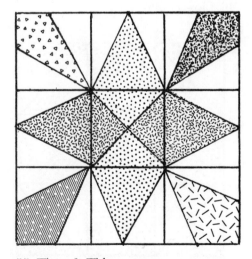

55 Time & Tide

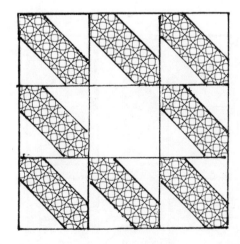

56 Nonesuch

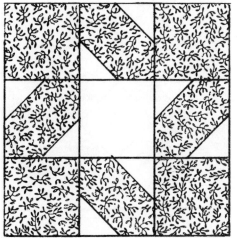

57 Mississippi

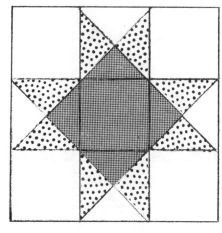

58 Variable Star

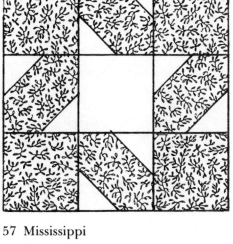

59 Ohio Star

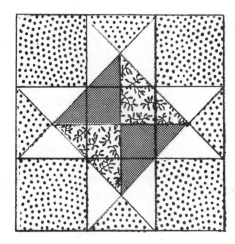

60 Country Farm

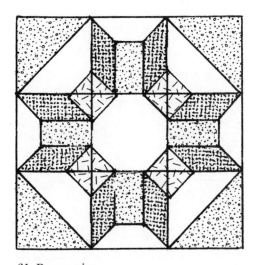

61 Prosperity

62 Card Basket

63 Braced Star I

64 Rhode Island

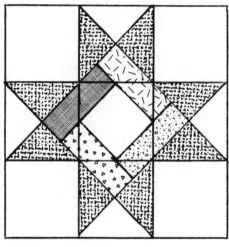

65 Braced Star II

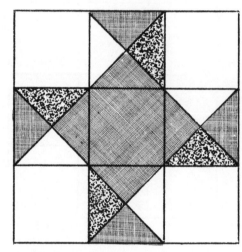

66 Stellie

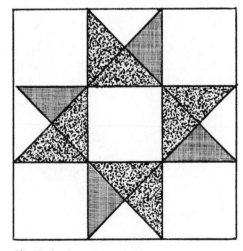

67 Twin Star

68 Ohio Star Variation

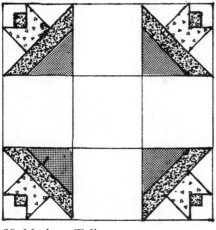

69 Modern Tulip

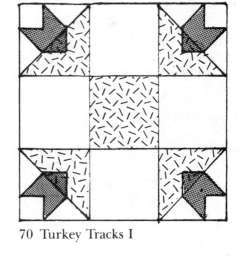

70 Turkey Tracks I

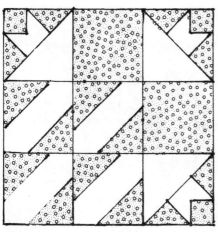

71 Tassel Plant

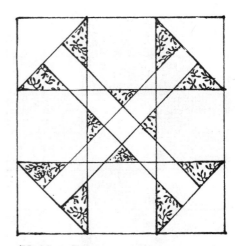

72 New Jersey

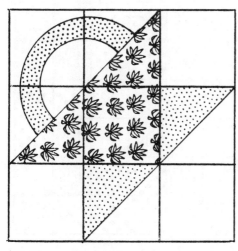

73 Flower Basket I

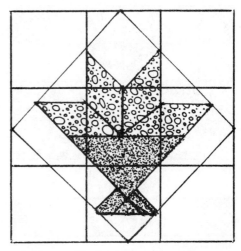

74 Cactus Basket

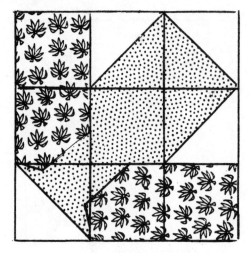

75 Goblet

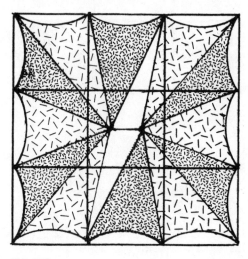

76 Wings

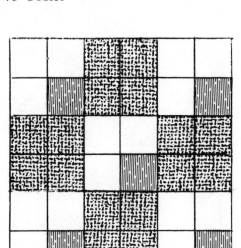

77 Pussy in the Corner

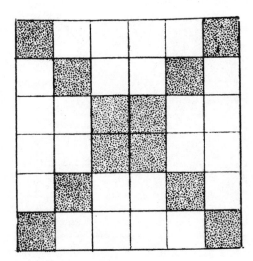

78 Pennsylvania I

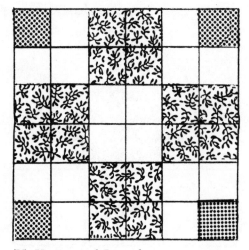

79 Homeward Bound

80 New Album I

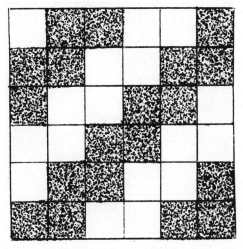

81 Streak of Lightning II

82 Postage Stamp

83 Patience Corner

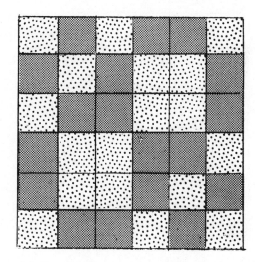

84 Domino I

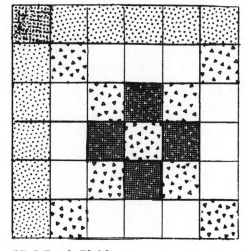

85 9-Patch Plaid

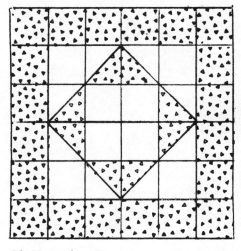

86 Hourglass II

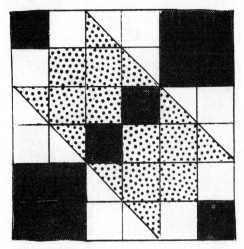

87 Broken Sugar Bowl

88 Road to the White House

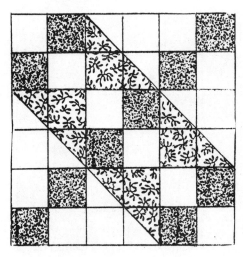

89 Jacob's Ladder I

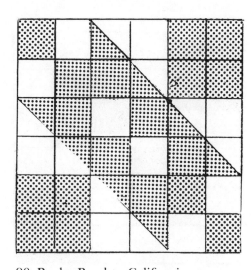

90 Rocky Road to California

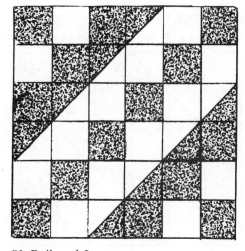

91 Railroad I

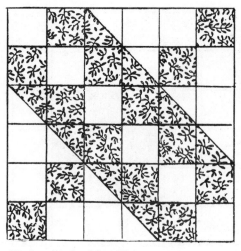

92 Jacob's Ladder II

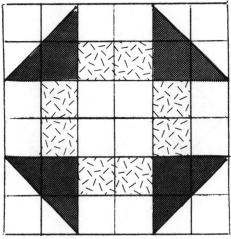

93 Churn Dash I

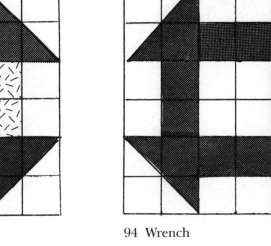

94 Wrench

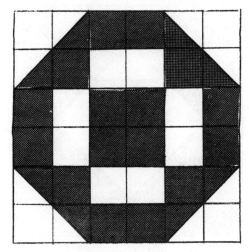

95 Grecian Design

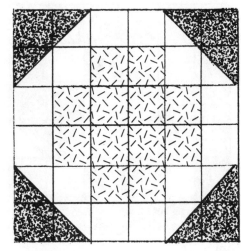

96 Greek Cross I

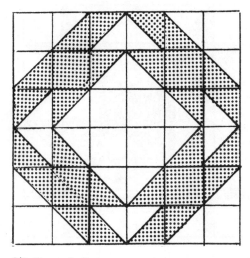

97 Cups & Saucers

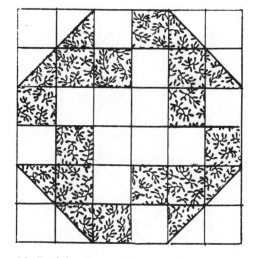

98 Prairie Queen I

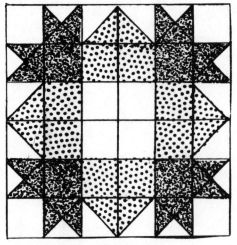

99 Weathervane Variation

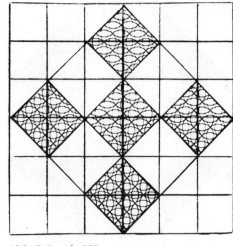

100 9-Patch III

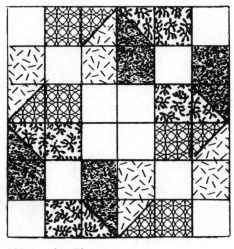

101 Lucky Clover

102 Garden Path I

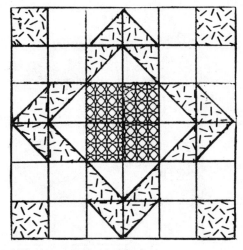

103 Aunt Sukey's Choice

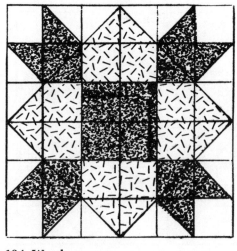

104 Weathervane

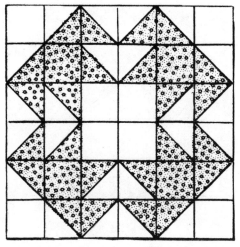

105 Capital T

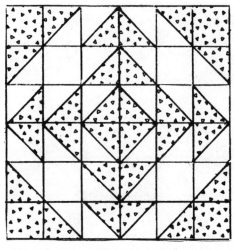

106 Illinois

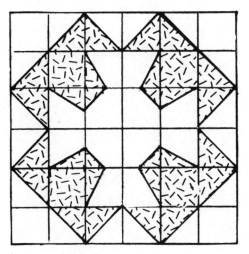

107 Imperial T

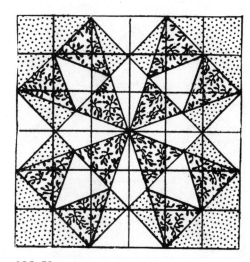

108 Vermont

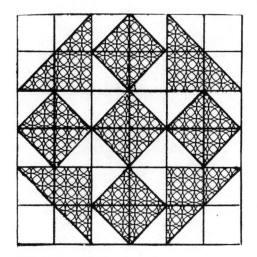

109 Sawtooth Patchwork

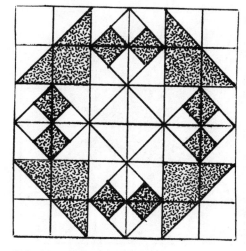

110 Aunt Vinah's Favorite

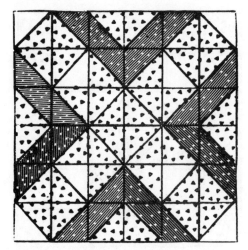

111 Saint George's Cross

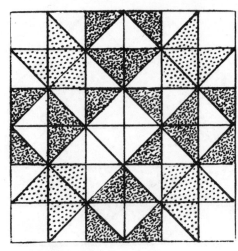

112 Indian Puzzle

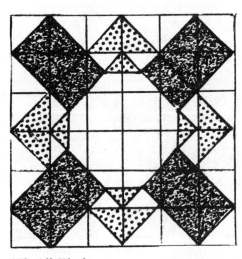

113 All Kinds

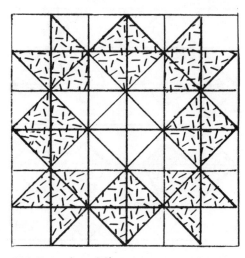

114 Love in a Mist

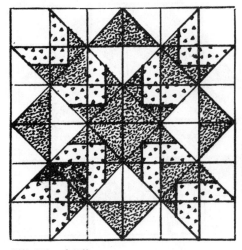

115 Wood Lily

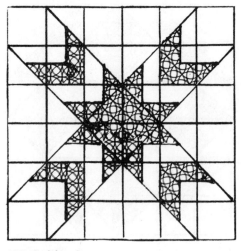

116 Spider Legs

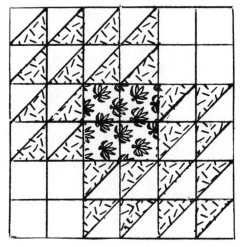

117 Winged Square I

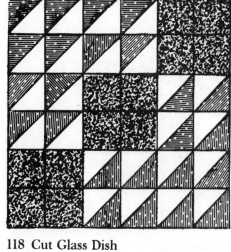

118 Cut Glass Dish

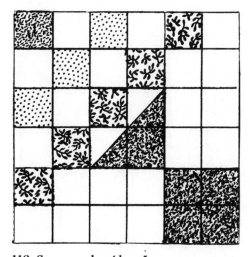

119 Steps to the Altar I

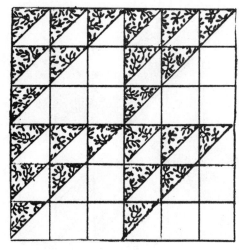

120 Birds in the Air II

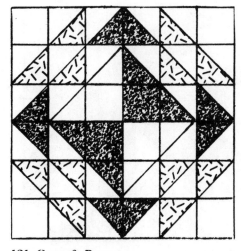

121 Corn & Beans

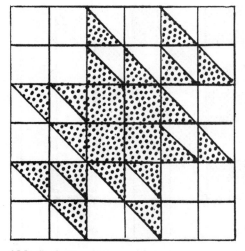

122 Cat's Cradle

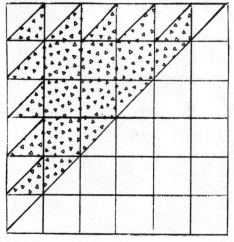

123 Sawtooth II

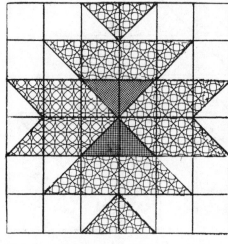

124 Squash Blossom

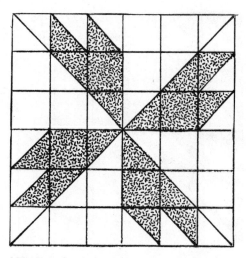

125 Rosebud I

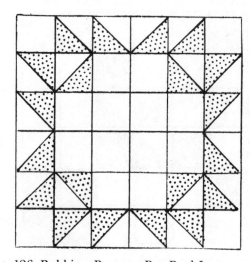

126 Robbing Peter to Pay Paul I

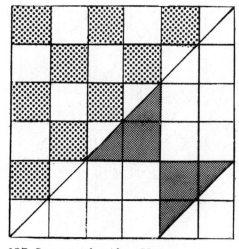

127 Steps to the Altar II

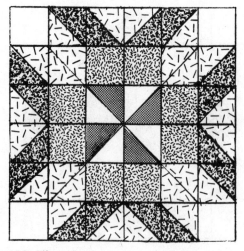

128 Silver Lane

129 Mother's Delight

130 St. Louis

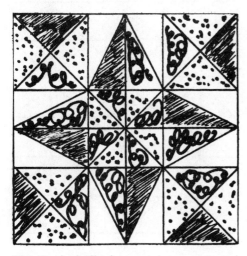

131 Optical Illusion

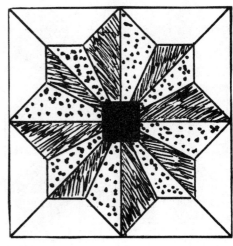

132 Sunbeam

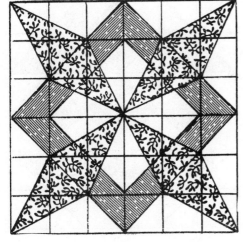

133 Barbara Bannister Star

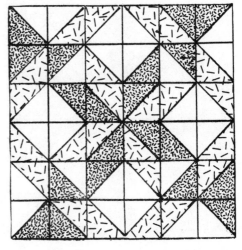

134 All Hallows

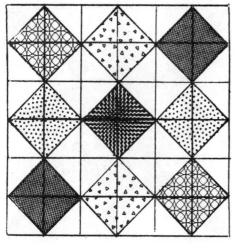

135 Checkerboard

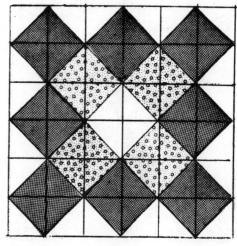

136 Courthouse Square

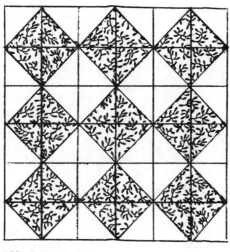

137 9-Patch IV

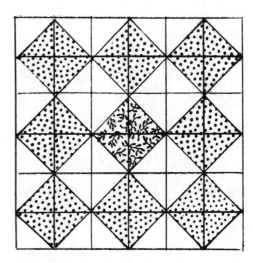

138 Arbor Window

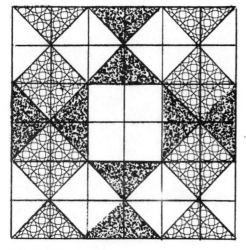

139 Jefferson City

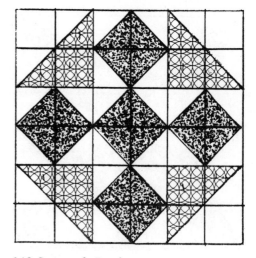

140 Sawtooth Patch

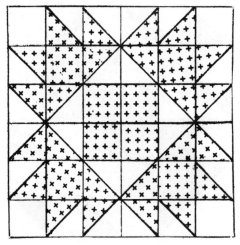

141 Union Square I

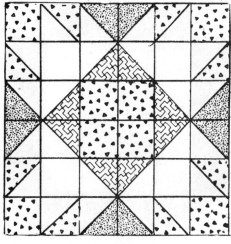

142 Union Square II

143 Contrary Wife II

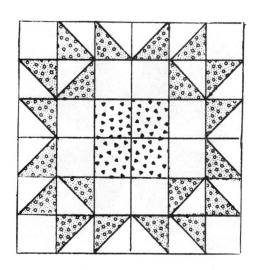

144 Arizona

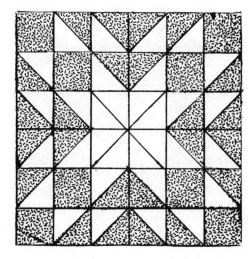

145 Star Gardner

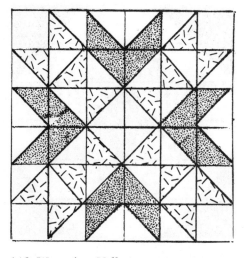

146 Wyoming Valley

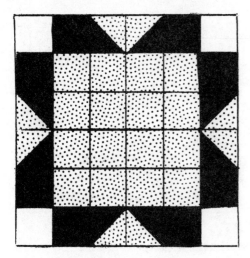

147 Square Dance

148 Kelly's Block

149 54-40 or Fight

150 Bird of Paradise

151 Doris's Delight

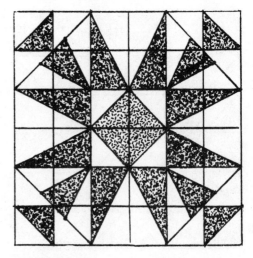

152 Rosebuds

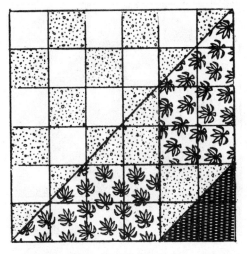

153 Strawberry Basket I

154 Strawberry Basket II

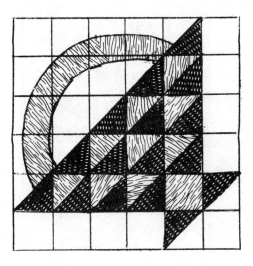

155 Basket I

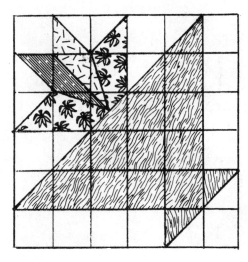

156 Flower Pot I

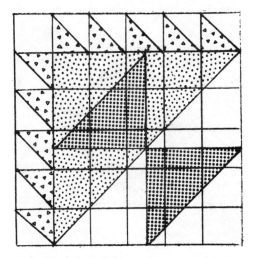

157 Birthday Cake

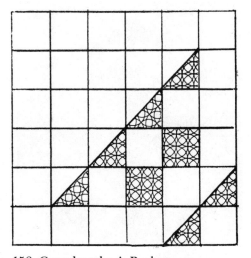

158 Grandmother's Basket

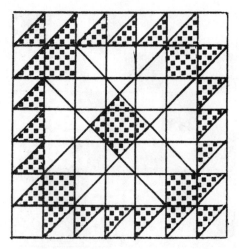

159 Queen Victoria's Crown

160 Mrs. Cleveland's Choice

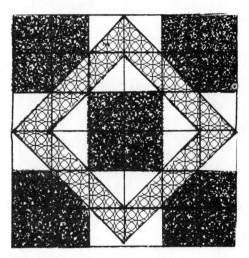

161 9-Patch Frame

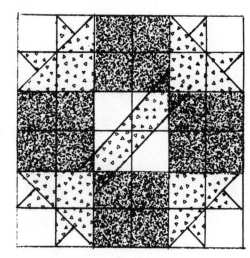

162 W.C.T.U.

163 Boxes

164 Handy Andy I

165 Flower Garden Path

166 Spider Web I

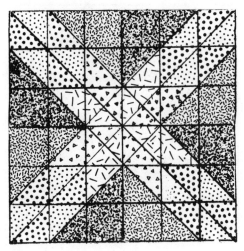

167 Patch as Patch Can

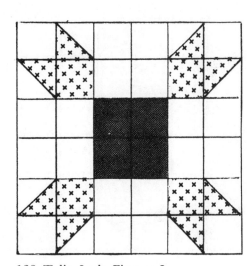

168 Tulip Lady Fingers I

169 Cross Variation

170 Swing in the Center I

49

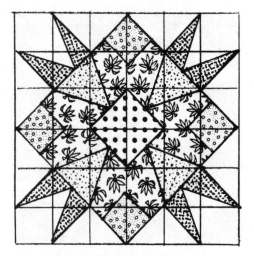

171 Winged Square II

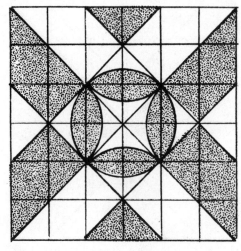

172 Dover Block

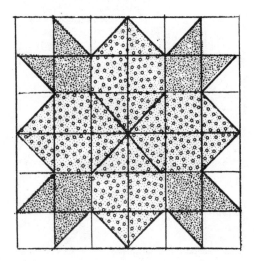

173 Morning

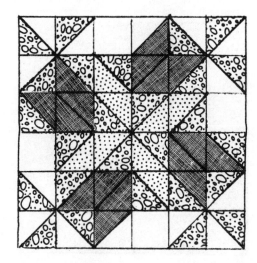

174 Four Winds

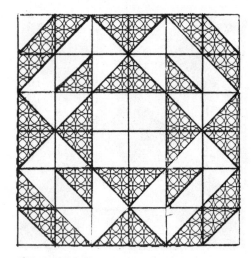

175 Jackknife

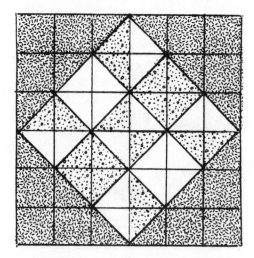

176 Storm Signal

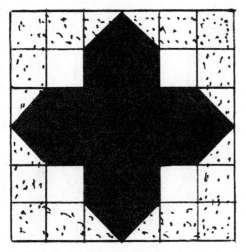

177 Grandmother's Own I

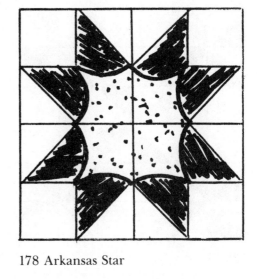

178 Arkansas Star

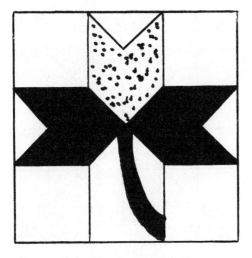

179 Sweet Gum Leaf

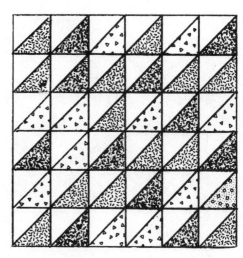

180 Battlegrounds

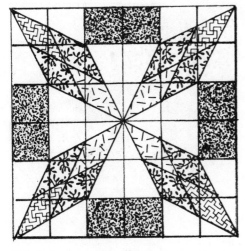

181 Arkansas Traveller I

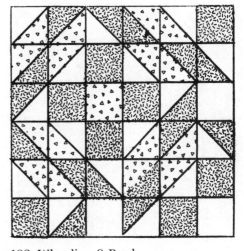

182 Wheeling 9-Patch

183 Flutterwheel

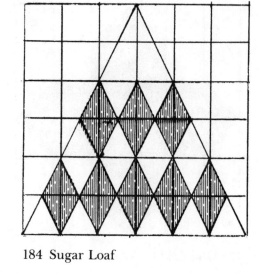

184 Sugar Loaf

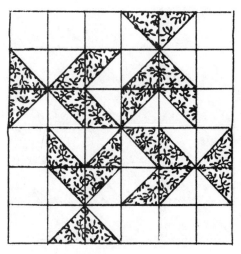

185 Flying Dutchman

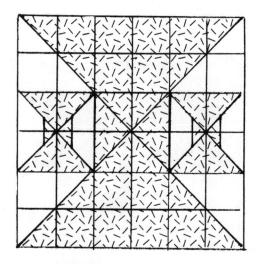

186 Spools III

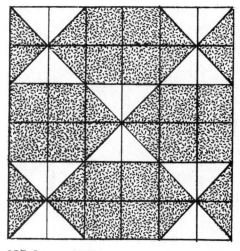

187 Letter-X II

188 Pine Tree I

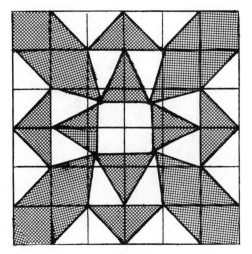

189 Annapolis Patch

190 Pinwheel Star I

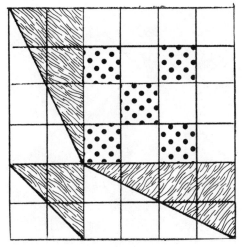

191 Nosegay I

192 Eight-Point Star I

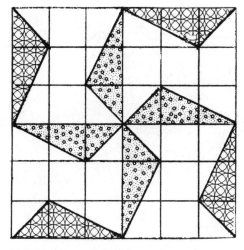

193 Walking Triangles

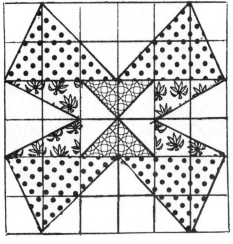

194 Bow

195 9-Patch Star II

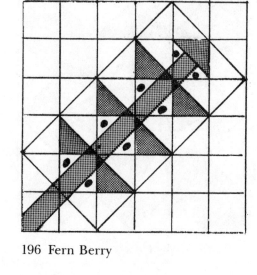

196 Fern Berry

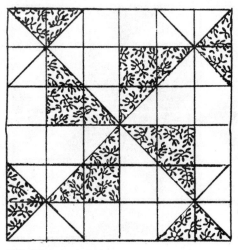

197 Ranger's Pride

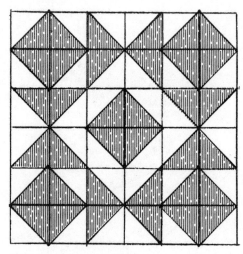

198 Combination Star

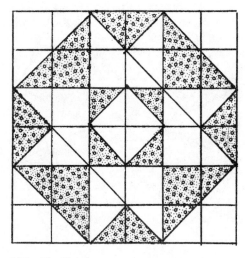

199 Air Castle

200 Entertaining Motions

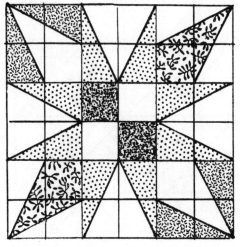

201 Claws

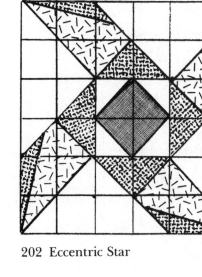

202 Eccentric Star

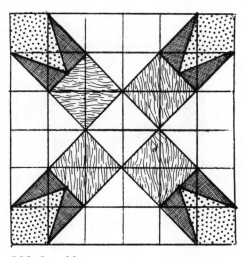

203 Sparkler

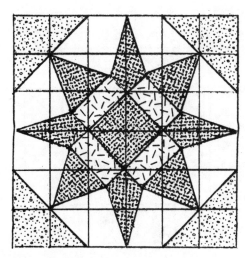

204 North Carolina Star

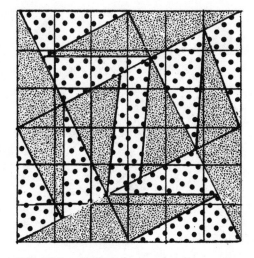

205 Triangle Puzzle

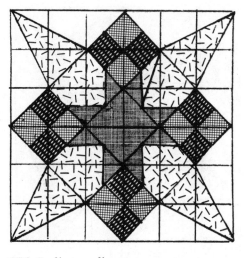

206 Indianapolis

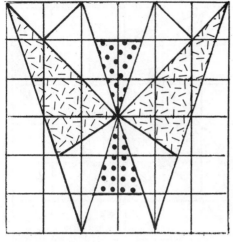

207 Butterfly I

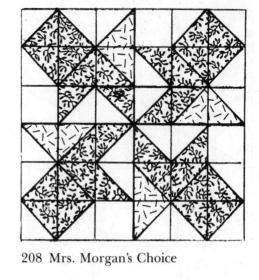

208 Mrs. Morgan's Choice

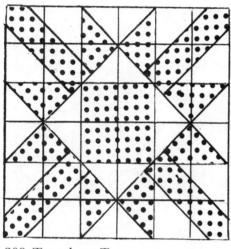

209 Turnabout-T

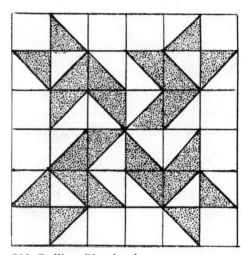

210 Rolling Pinwheel

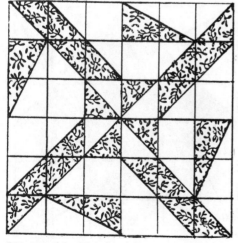

211 Double Pinwheel I

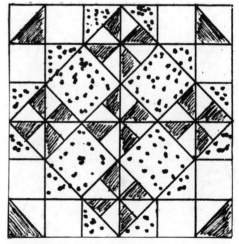

212 South Dakota

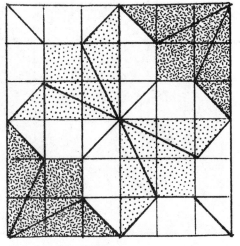

213 Double Tulip

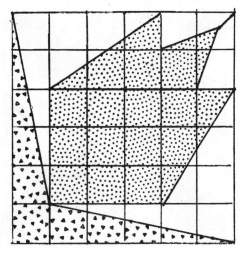

214 Tulip I

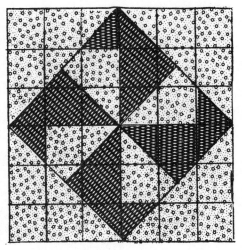

215 Wheeling Triangles

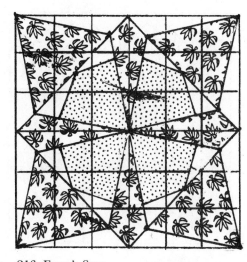

216 Exea's Star

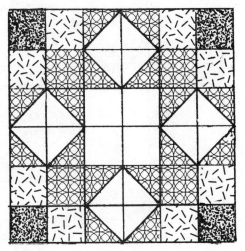

217 No Name Patch

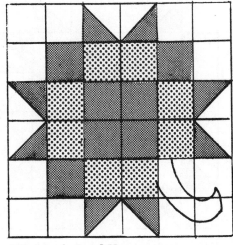

218 Maple Leaf II

219 Ribbons I

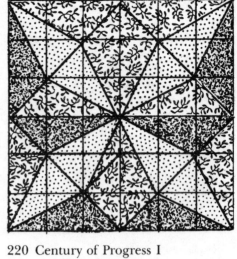

220 Century of Progress I

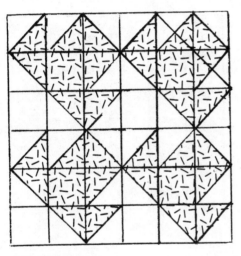

221 T-Quartette

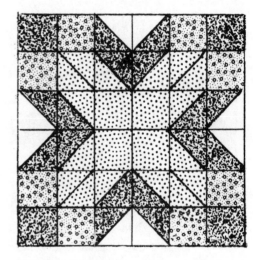

222 Merry Kite

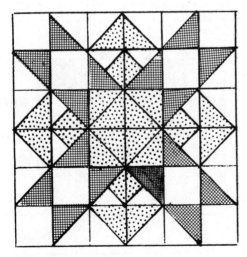

223 Christmas Star

224 Morning Star I

58

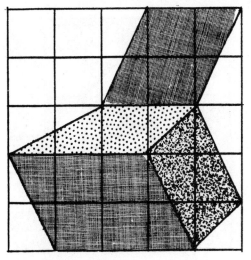

225 Workbox

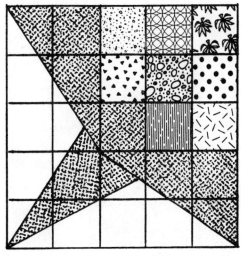

226 Crazy Quilt Bouquet

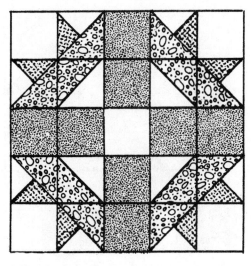

227 Mexican Star

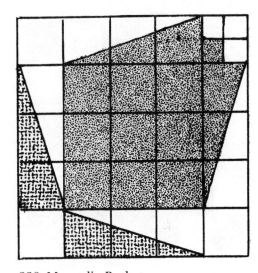

228 Magnolia Bud

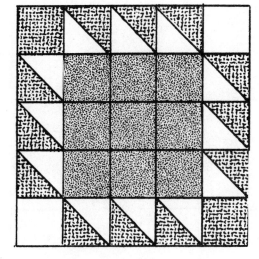

229 Double Sawtooth I

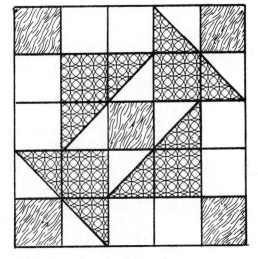

230 Grandmother's Puzzle

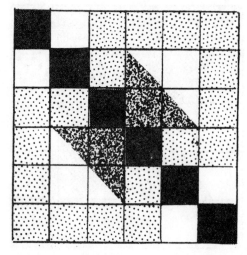

231 Hayes's Corners

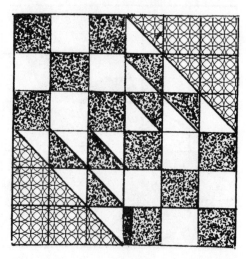

232 Battle of the Alamo

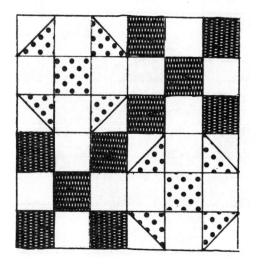

233 Tic Tac Toe

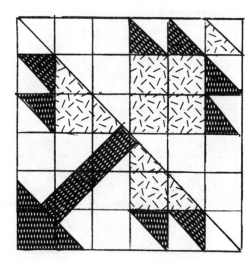

234 English Ivy

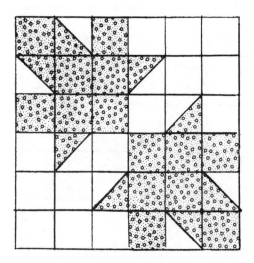

235 Ozark Maple Leaf

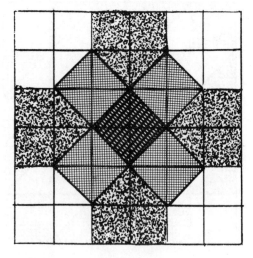

236 California

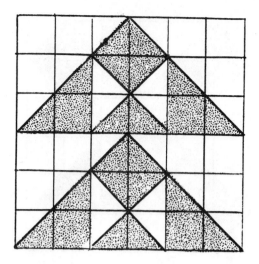

237 Hill & Valley

238 Virginia Reel

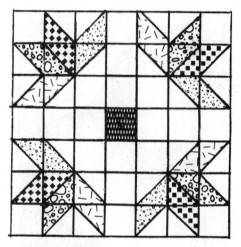

239 Fancy Flowers

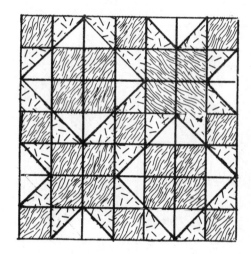

240 Road to California I

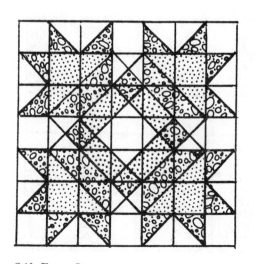

241 Four Queens

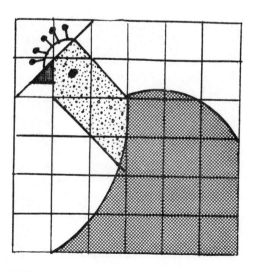

242 Peacock

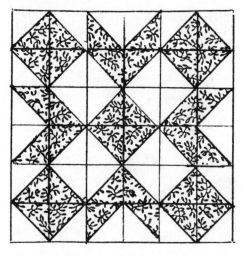

243 Swing in the Center II

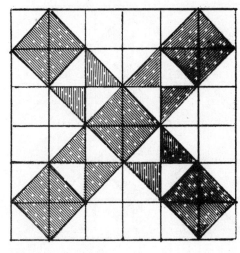

244 Cats & Mice I

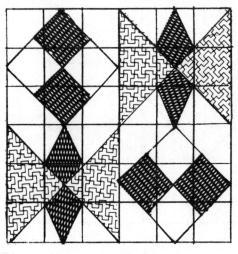

245 Conventional Block

246 Flutterbye

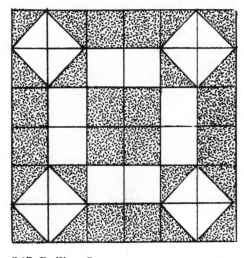

247 Rolling Stone

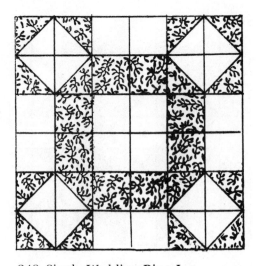

248 Single Wedding Ring I

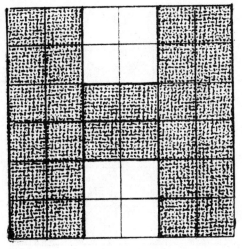

249 H-Block

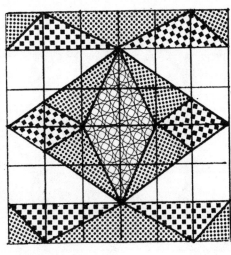

250 Shooting Star I

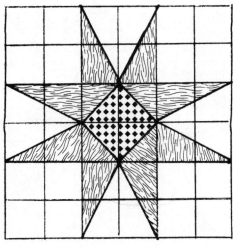

251 Pineapple

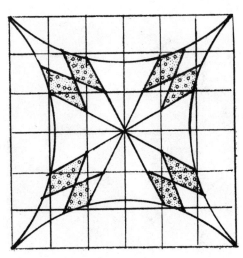

252 Arab Tent

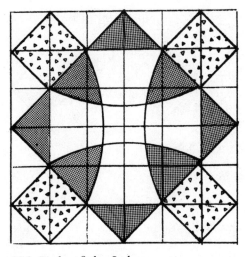

253 Lady of the Lake

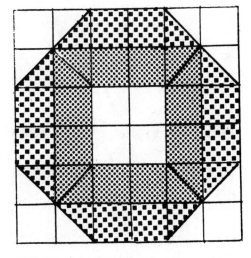

254 Kitchen Woodbox

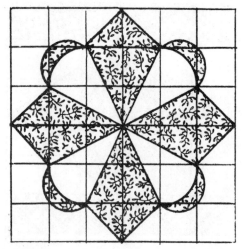

255 Star & Crescent

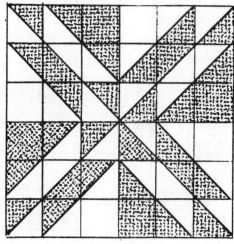

256 Gretchen

257 Hopscotch

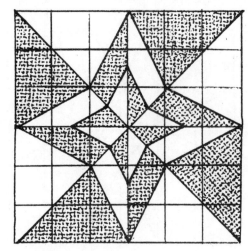

258 Night & Day

259 Guiding Star

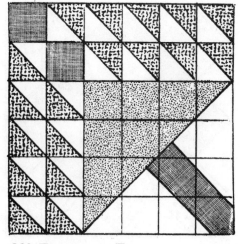

260 Temperance Tree

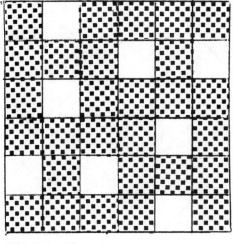

261 Four-H

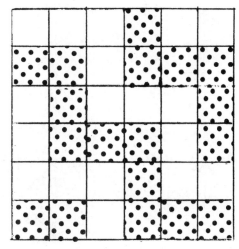

262 London Stairs II

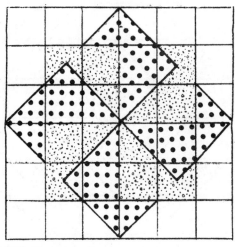

263 Twisting Star

264 Colonial Rose

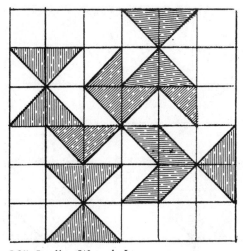

265 Ladies Wreath I

266 Dumbell Block

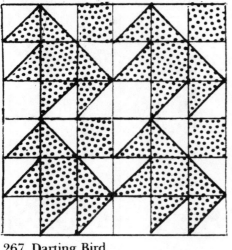

267 Darting Bird

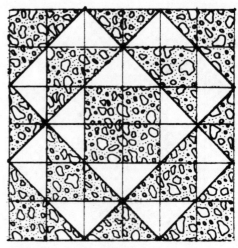

268 Gentleman's Fancy

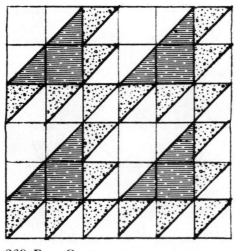

269 Four Crowns

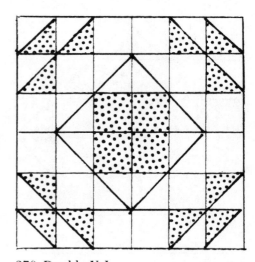

270 Double-X I

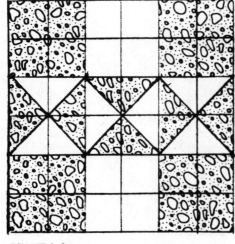

271 Triplet

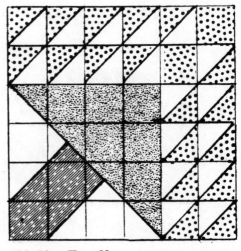

272 Pine Tree II

273 Montana

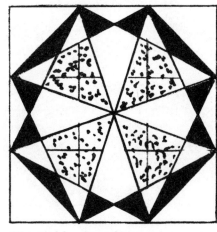

274 Golda, Gem Star

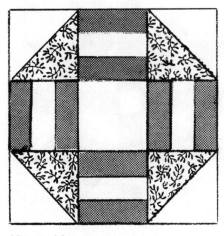

275 Golden Gate

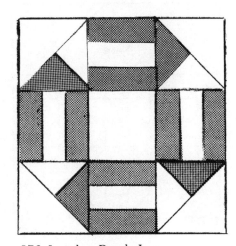

276 London Roads I

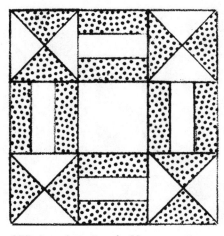

277 London Roads II

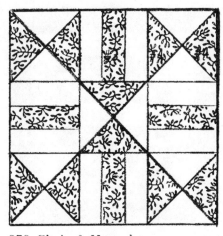

278 Chain & Hourglass

279 Farmer's Puzzle

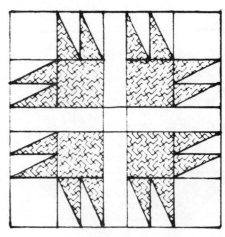

280 Turkey Tracks II

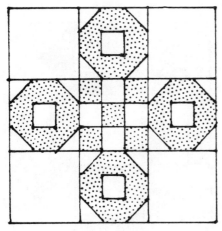

281 Santa Fe

282 Continental I

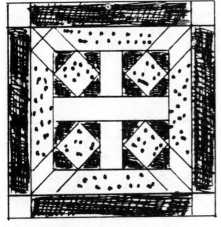

283 Arkansas I

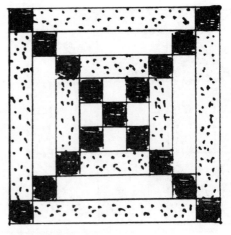

284 Alabama

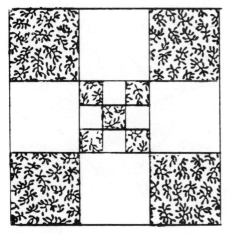

285 Double 9-Patch

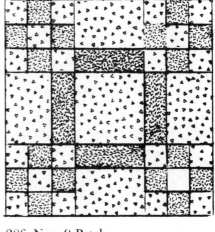

286 New 9-Patch

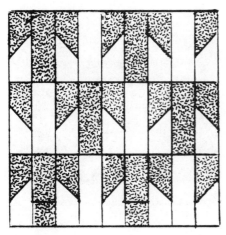

287 Mixed T

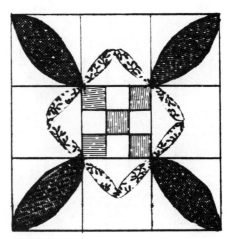

288 Blue Blazes

289 Patchwork Posy

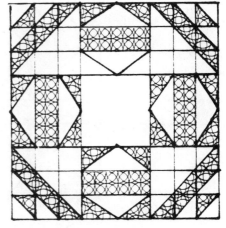

290 Mollie's Choice

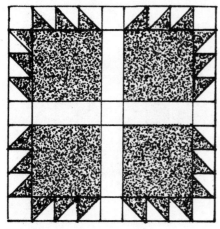

291 Premium Star

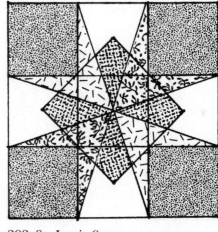

292 St. Louis Star

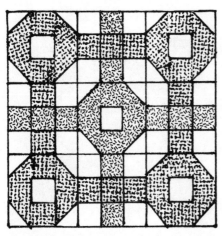

293 Tile Puzzle

294 Log Cabin I

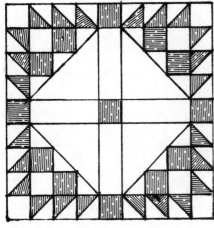

295 Bear's Den

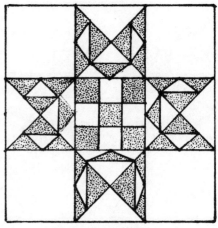

296 Dolly Madison Star

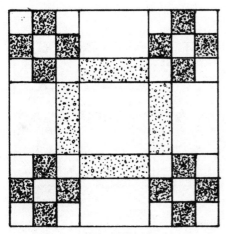

297 Puss in the Corner I

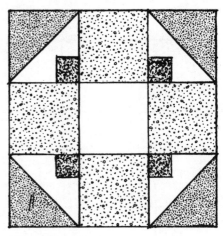

298 Album I

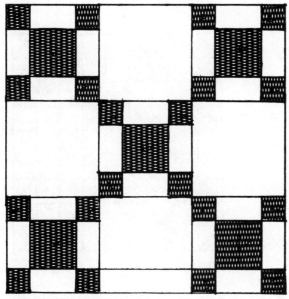

299 Puss in the Corner II

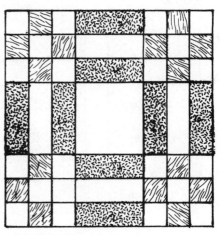

300 Building Blocks

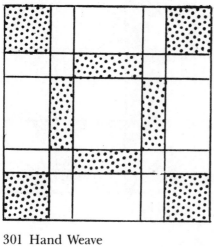

301 Hand Weave

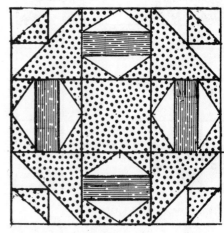

302 Joseph's Coat I

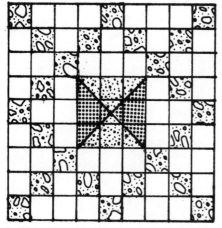

303 Crosspatch

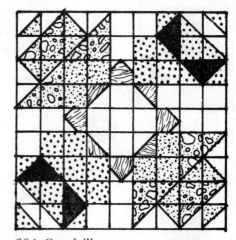

304 Quadrille

305 City Streets

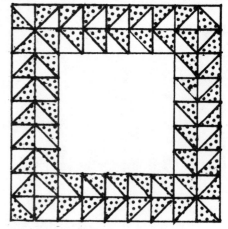

306 Wandering Lanes

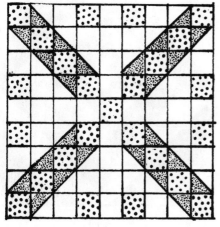

307 Dublin Chain

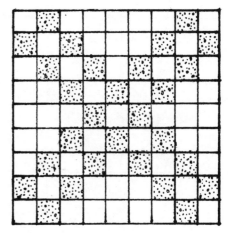

308 Garden Path II

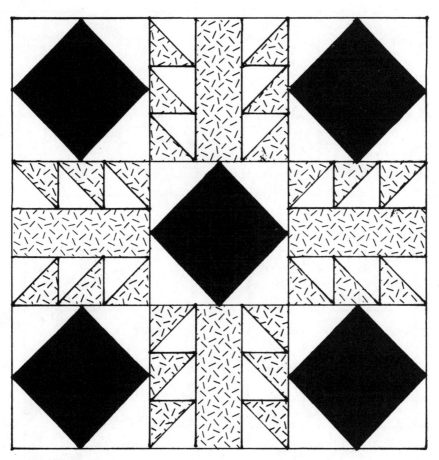

309 Mother's Dream I

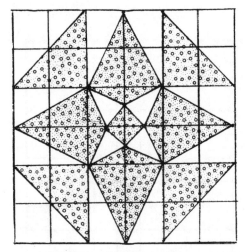

310 Little Rock Block

311 Merry-Go-Round I

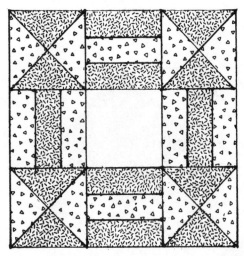

312 At the Square

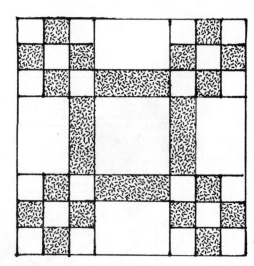

313 9-Patch V

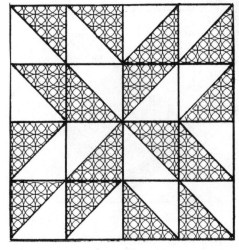

314 Annie's Choice

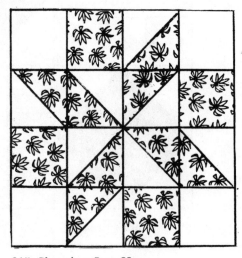

315 Shooting Star II

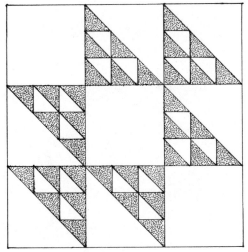

316 Double Pyramid

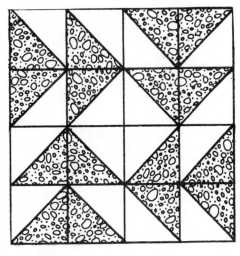

317 Mosaic I

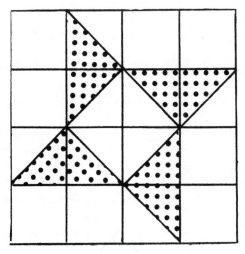

318 Pinwheel Askew

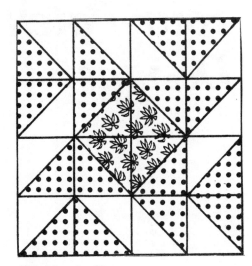

319 Mosaic #9

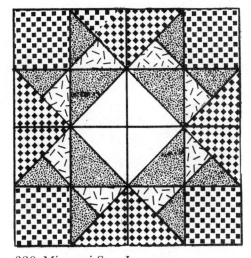

320 Missouri Star I

Four-Patch Designs

2″ = 4″ block
3″ = 6″ block
4″ = 8″ block
5″ = 10″ block
6″ = 12″ block
7″ = 14″ block
8″ = 16″ block
9″ = 18″ block

4-Patch

2″ = 8″ block
3″ = 12″ block
4″ = 16″ block
5″ = 20″ block

4-Patch
Divided in Half

1″ = 8″ block
2″ = 16″ block
3″ = 24″ block

4-Patch
Divided into Fourths

321 4-Patch

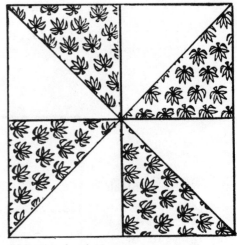

322 Pinwheel II

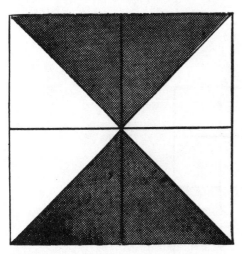

323 Cotton Reel

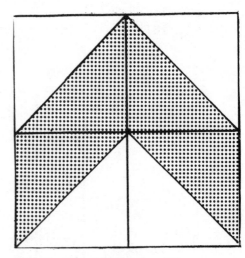

324 Streak of Lightning III

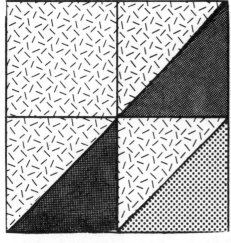

325 Birds ın the Air III

326 Big Dipper

327 Broken Dishes I

328 Broken Pinwheel

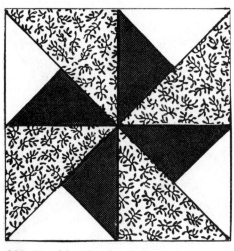

329 Double Pinwheel II

330 Turnstile

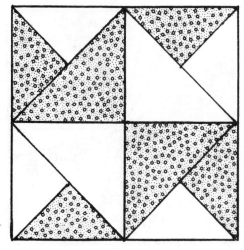

331 Southern Belle

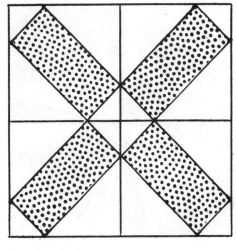

332 Devil's Puzzle

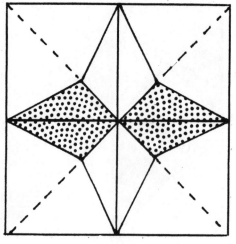

333 Periwinkle

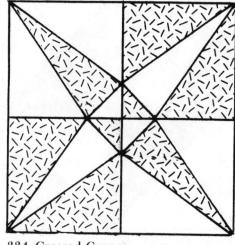

334 Crossed Canoes

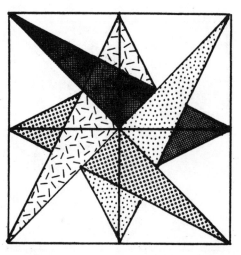

335 Laced Star

336 Southern Star

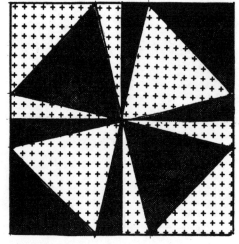

337 Shoemaker's Puzzle

338 Endless Chain

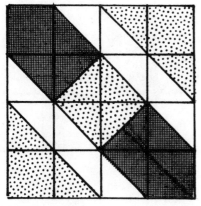

339 Red Cross II

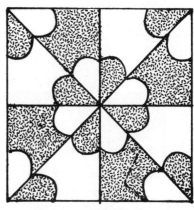

340 Borrow & Return

341 Twist & Turn

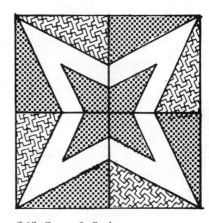

342 Stars & Stripes

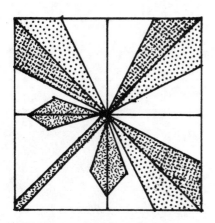

343 State of Ohio

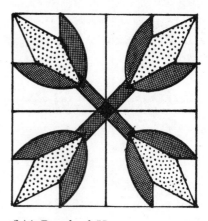

344 Rosebud II

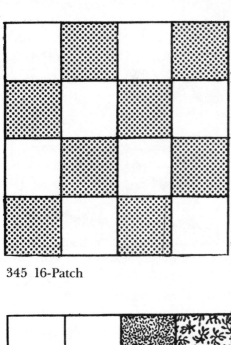

345 16-Patch

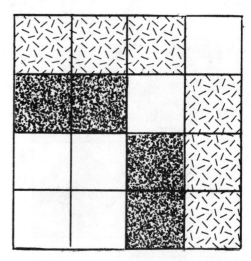

346 Scot's Plaid

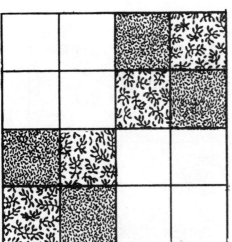

347 4-Patch Variation

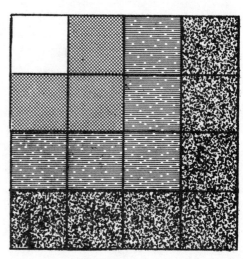

348 Rainbow Flower

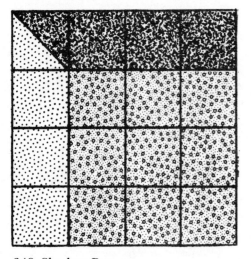

349 Shadow Box

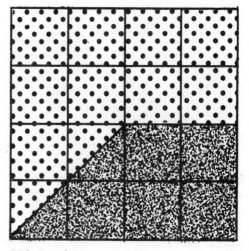

350 Jewel I

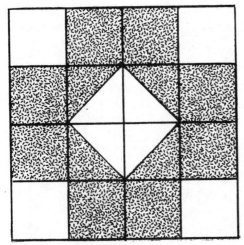

351 Susannah I

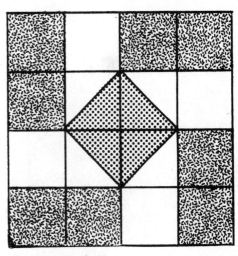

352 Susannah II

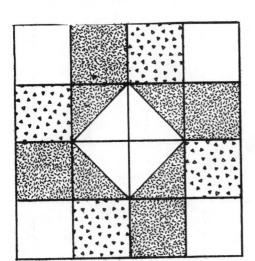

353 Susannah III

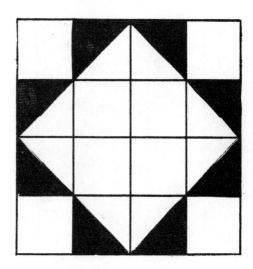

354 Art Square

355 New Album II

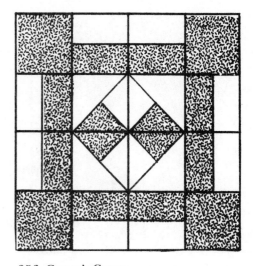

356 Coxey's Camp

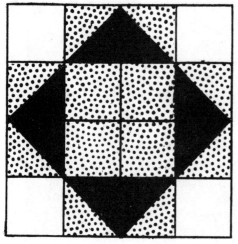

357 Album II

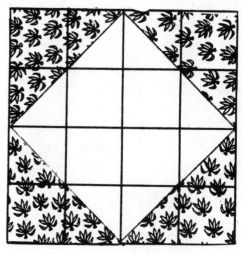

358 Shoofly II

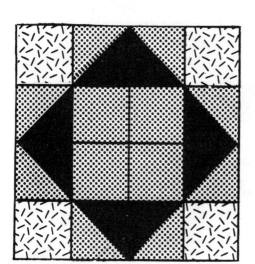

359 King's Crown I

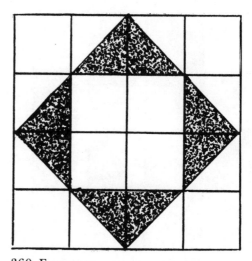

360 Economy

361 Twelve Triangles

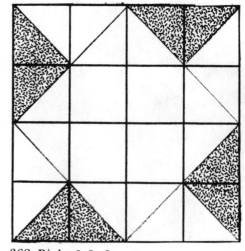

362 Right & Left

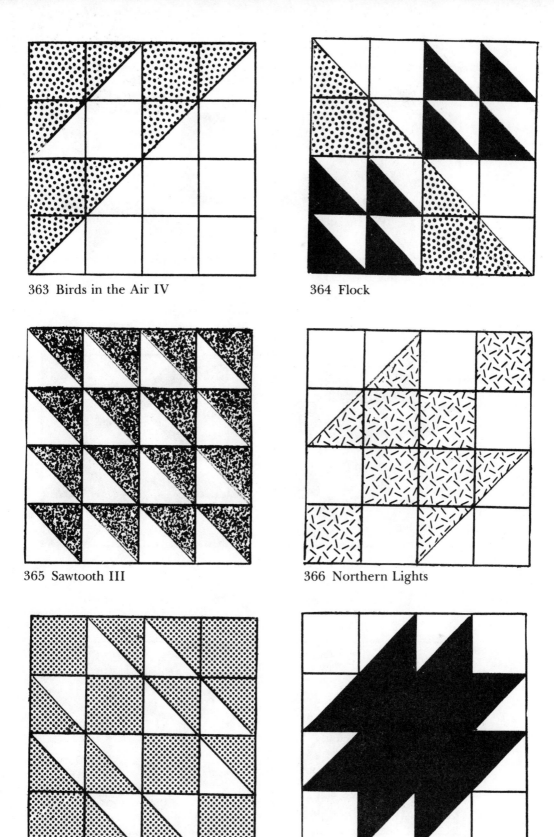

363 Birds in the Air IV

364 Flock

365 Sawtooth III

366 Northern Lights

367 Hovering Hawks

368 Anvil

369 Eight-Point Star II

370 Evening Star

371 Stars & Squares

372 Star I

373 Tippecanoe & Tyler Too

374 8-Hands Around

375 The Seasons

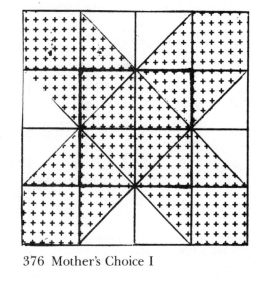

376 Mother's Choice I

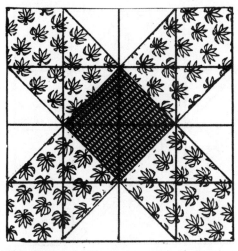

377 Pointed Tile

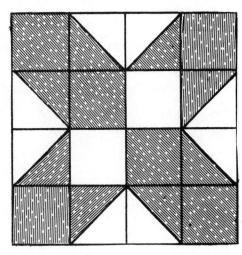

378 Indian Star

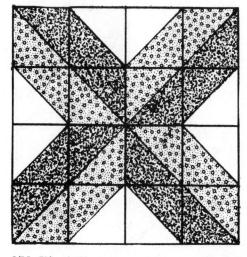

379 King's X

380 Primrose Path I

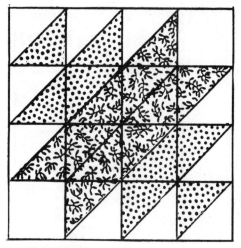

381 Mrs. Taft's Choice

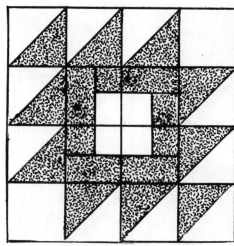

382 Rocky Mountain Puzzle

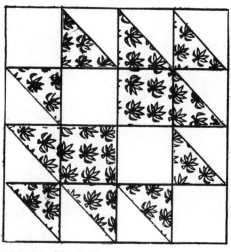

383 Double-X II

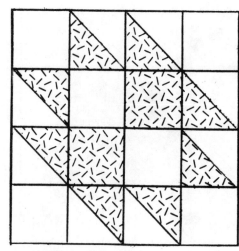

384 Double-X III

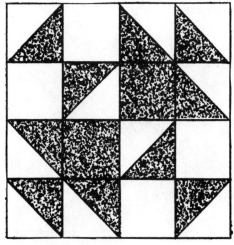

385 Old Maid's Puzzle

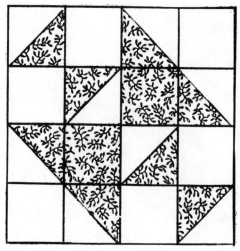

386 Crosses & Losses

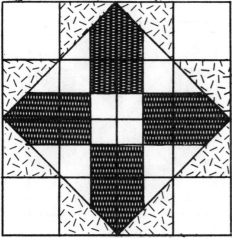

387 Cross in a Cross

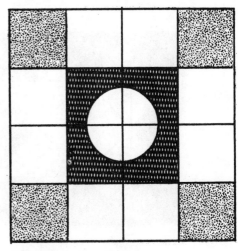

388 Circle in a Frame

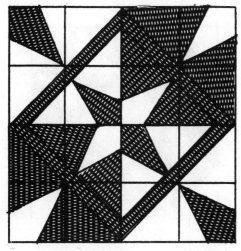

389 Small Business

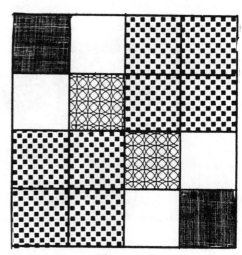

390 Autumn Tints

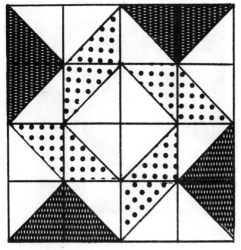

391 Balkan Puzzle

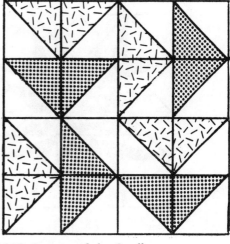

392 Return of the Swallows

89

393 Missouri Star II

394 Martha Washington Star

395 Mother's Choice II

396 Star II

397 Missouri Star III

398 Star III

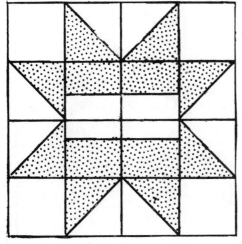

399 Album Star

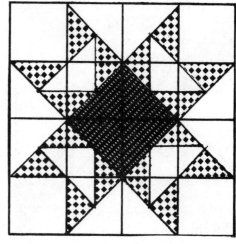

400 Northumberland Star

401 French Star

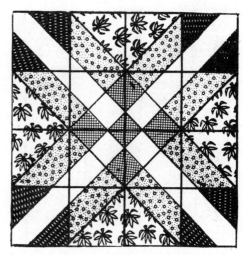

402 Mexican Cross I

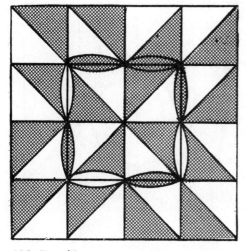

403 Fox Chase

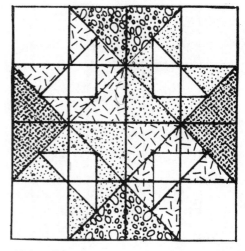

404 Wild Geese

405 Trailing Star

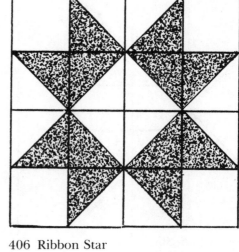

406 Ribbon Star

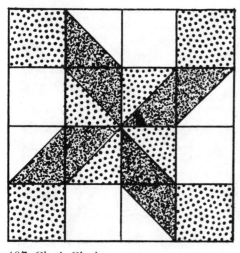

407 Clay's Choice

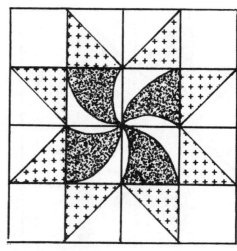

408 Pinwheel Star II

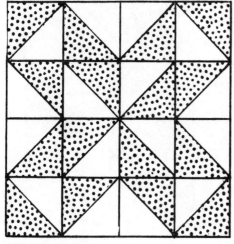

409 Pierced Star

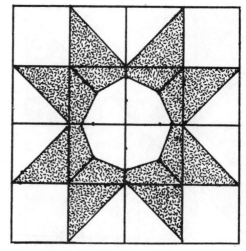

410 Missouri Daisy

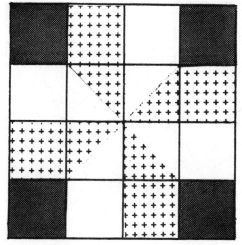

411 Nelson's Victory

412 Windows (diagonal set)

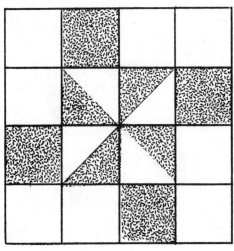

413 Windmill I

414 Arkansas Crossroads

415 Road to Oklahoma I

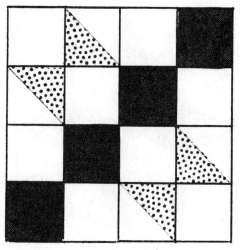

416 Road to Oklahoma II

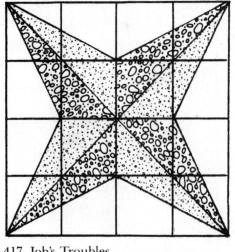

417 Job's Troubles

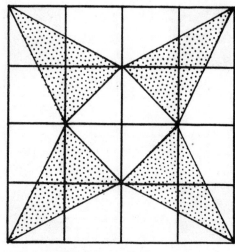

418 World Without End

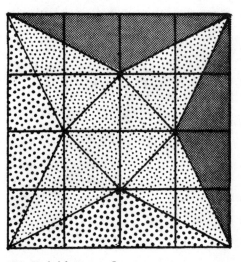

419 Kaleidoscope I

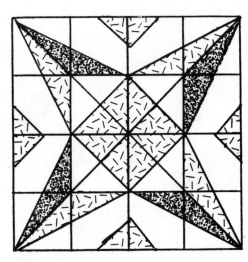

420 World's Fair

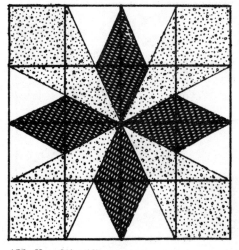

421 Key West Star

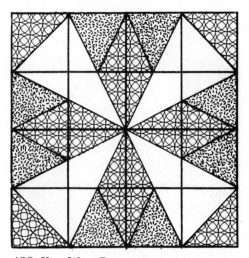

422 Key West Beauty

423 Aunt Eliza's Star

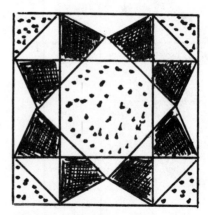

424 Peaceful Hours

425 No Name

426 Pennsylvania II

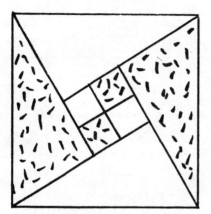

427 Arabic Lattice

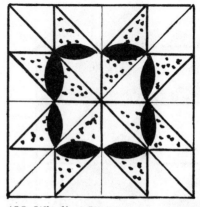

428 Winding Walk

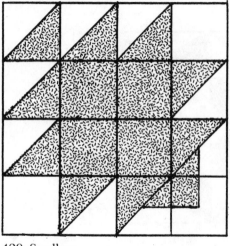

429 Swallow

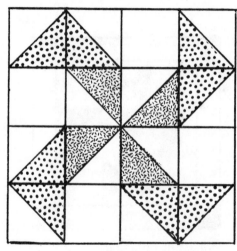

430 Seesaw

431 Spinner

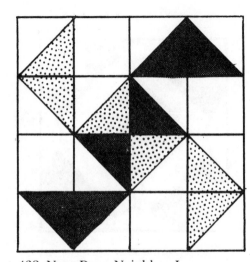

432 Next Door Neighbor I

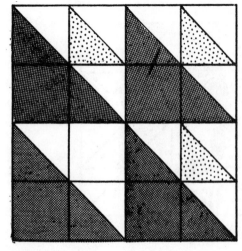

433 Aircraft

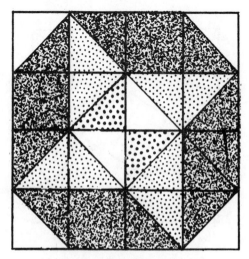

434 Next Door Neighbor II

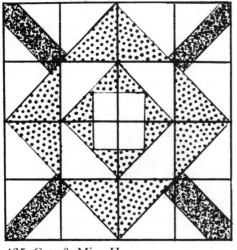

435 Cats & Mice II

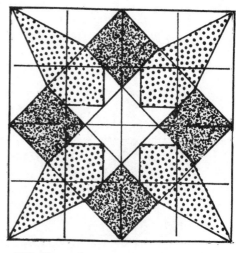

436 Skyrocket

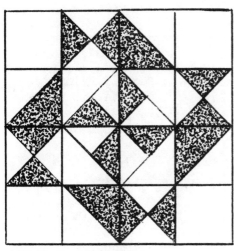

437 Catch as You Can

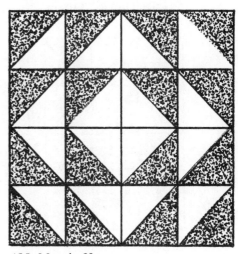

438 Mosaic II

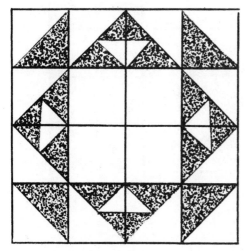

439 Grandmother's Own

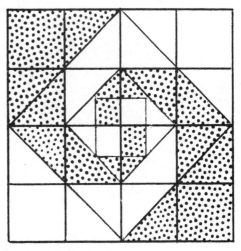

440 Indian Puzzle

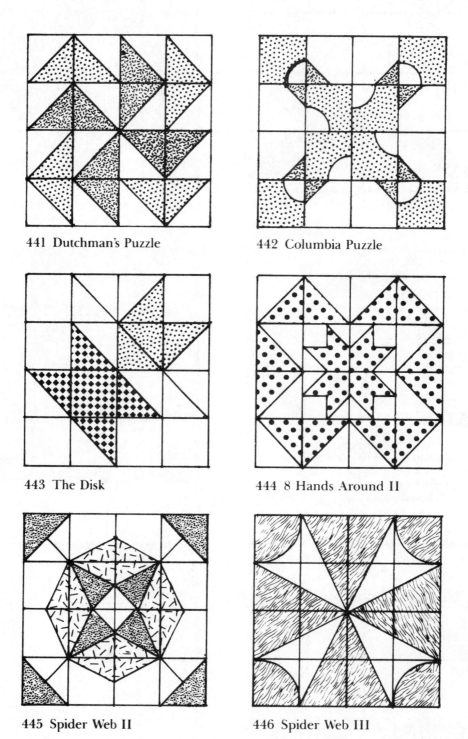

441 Dutchman's Puzzle

442 Columbia Puzzle

443 The Disk

444 8 Hands Around II

445 Spider Web II

446 Spider Web III

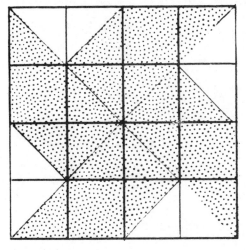

447 Whirlwind

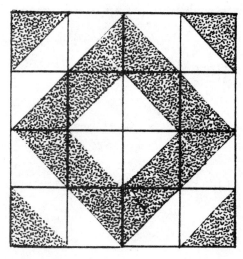

448 Fancy Stripe

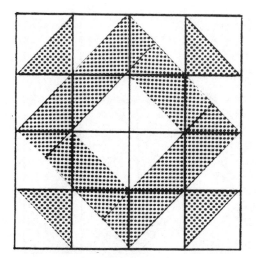

449 Broken Dishes II

450 Four Points

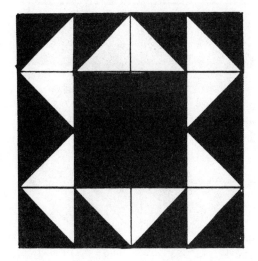

451 Buzzard's Roost

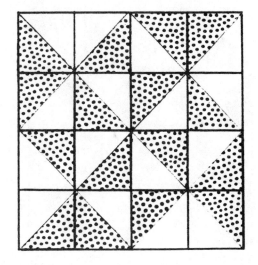

452 Peace & Plenty

453 Broken Dishes III

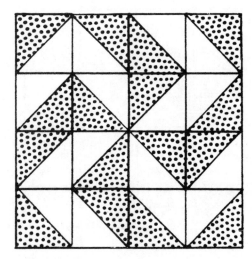

454 Louisiana

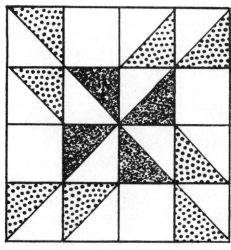

455 Year's Favorite

456 Swastika I

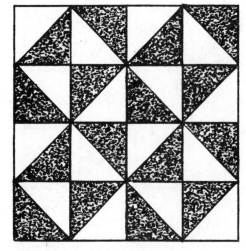

457 Broken Dishes IV

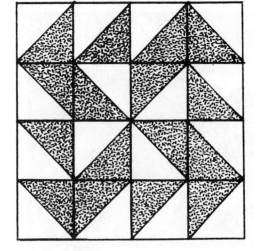

458 Yankee Puzzle

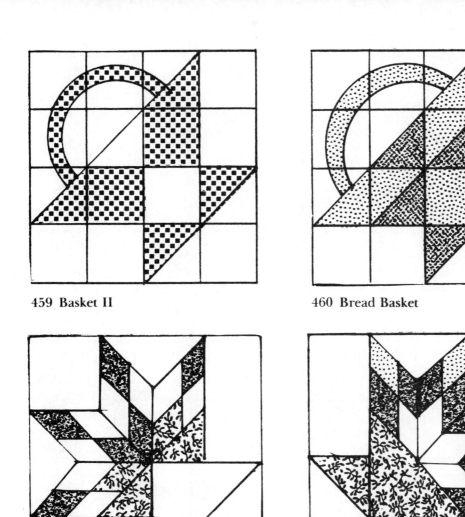

459 Basket II

460 Bread Basket

461 Flower Pot II

462 Tulip Basket

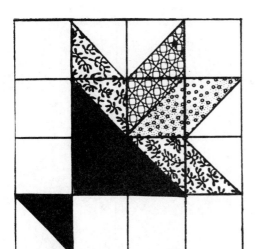

463 Bouquet

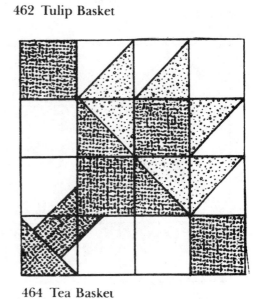

464 Tea Basket

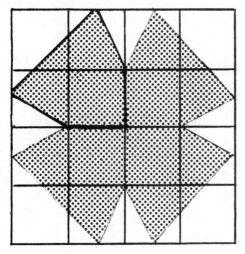

465 Mayflower

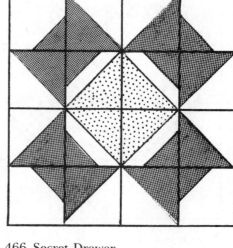

466 Secret Drawer

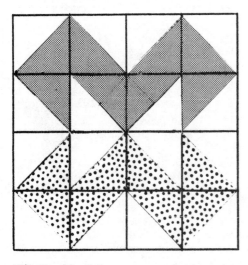

467 Double-Z I

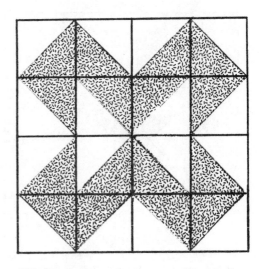

468 Hourglass III

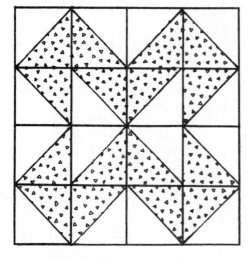

469 Double-Z II

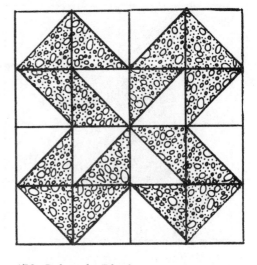

470 Colorado Block

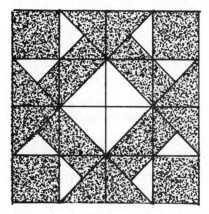

471 Centennial II

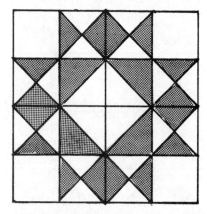

472 Square & Star

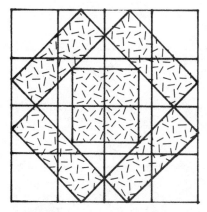

473 Boy's Nonsense

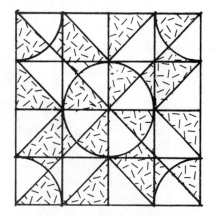

474 Square & Compass

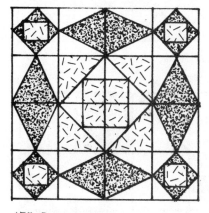

475 Storm at Sea

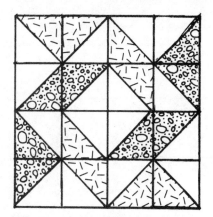

476 Windblown Square

477 Mill & Star

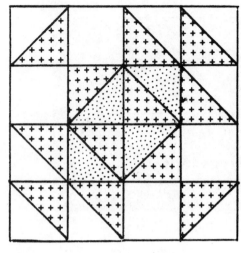

478 Flying Dutchman II

479 Chinese Puzzle

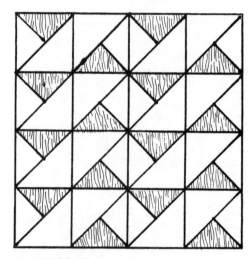

480 Wild Waves

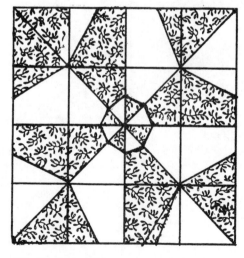

481 Turkey Giblets

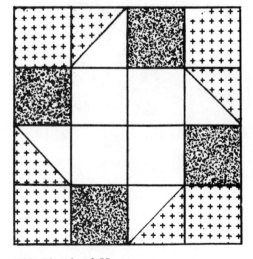

482 Pinwheel II

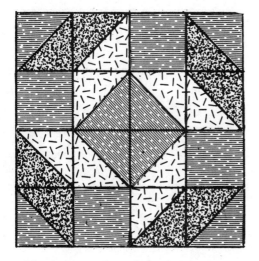

483 Bachelor's Puzzle I

484 End of Day

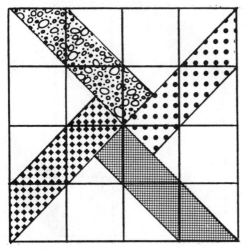

485 Windmill II

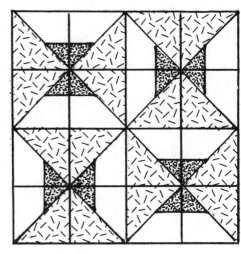

486 Arkansas Traveller II

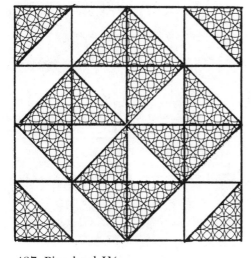

487 Pinwheel III

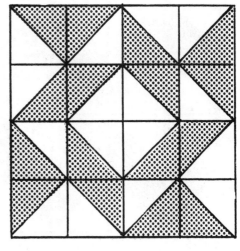

488 Whirlpool

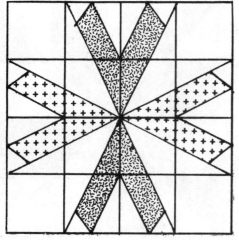

489 V-Block I

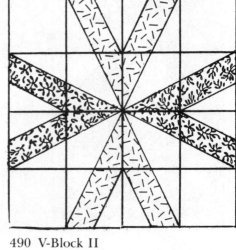

490 V-Block II

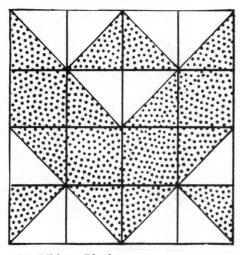

491 Ribbon Block

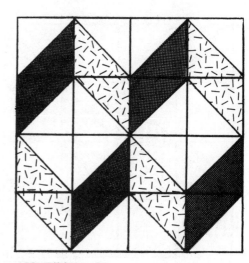

492 Ribbons II

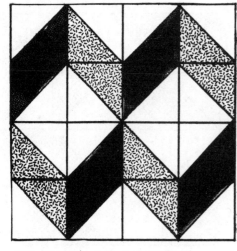

493 Grandma's Red & White

494 Maltese Cross

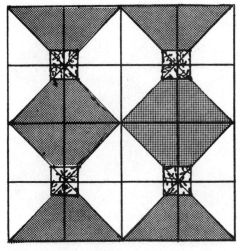

495 Grandmother's Own III

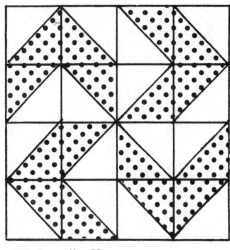

496 Swastika II

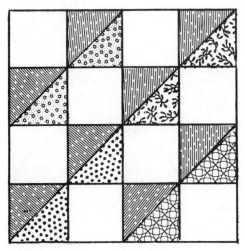

497 Cotton Reels

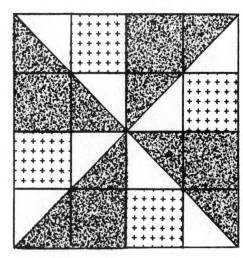

498 Brave World

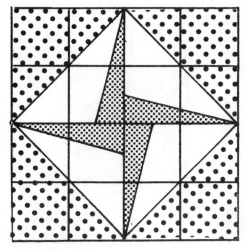

499 Waste Not

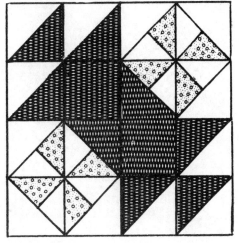

500 Hither & Yon

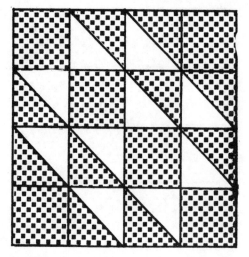

501 Hovering Birds

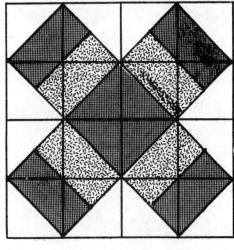

502 Mother's Dream II

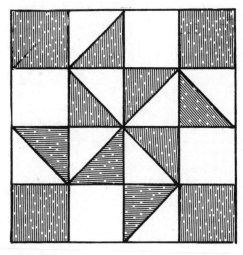

503 Flying-X

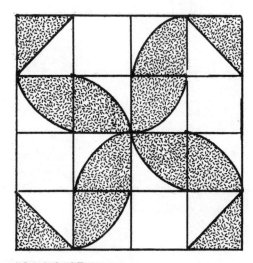

504 Windflower

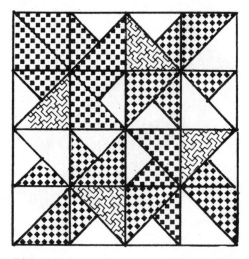

505 Windmill III

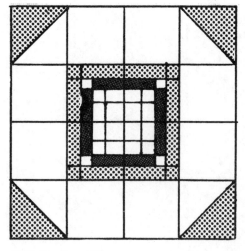

506 Yankee Charm

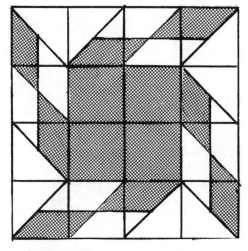

507 Flying Bats

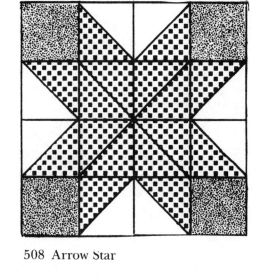

508 Arrow Star

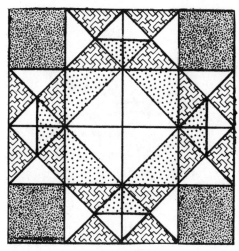

509 Crown of Thorns

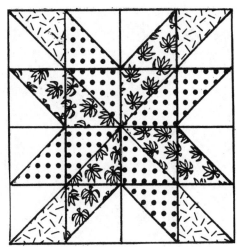

510 Constellation

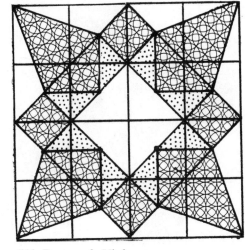

511 Dogtooth Violet

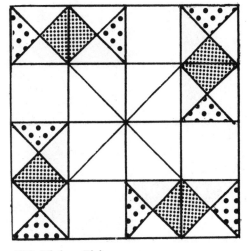

512 Flying Fish

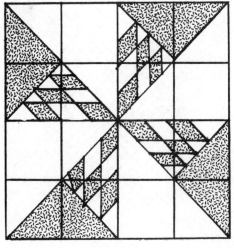

513 Dutch Windmill

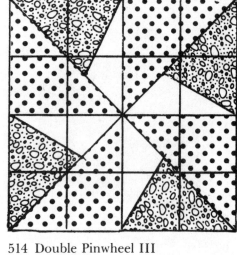

514 Double Pinwheel III

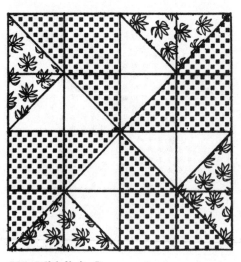

515 Whirligig I

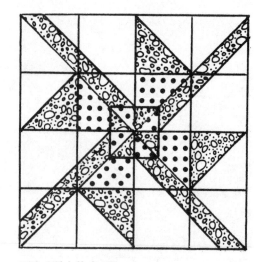

516 Whirligig II

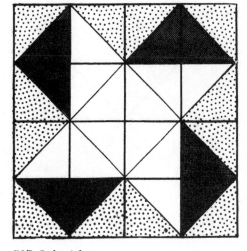

517 July 4th

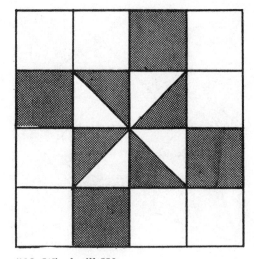

518 Windmill IV

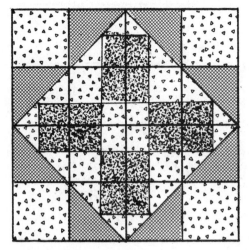

519 Cross Within Cross

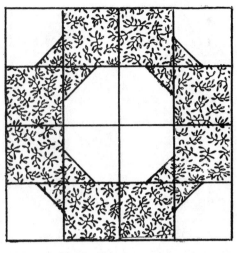

520 Magic Circle

521 Posy Patch

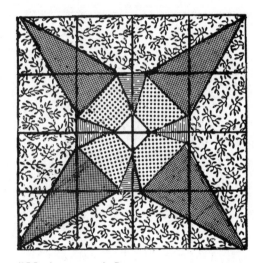

522 Annamae's Star

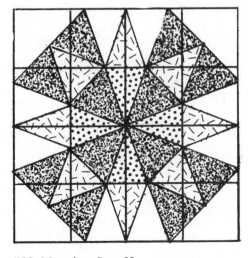

523 Morning Star II

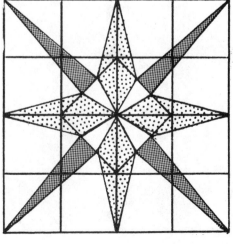

524 Star & Cone

111

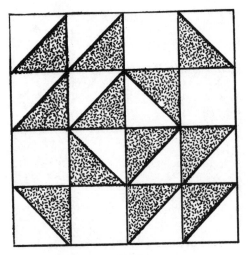

525 Ladies Wreath II

526 Pinwheel IV

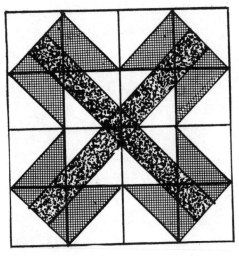

527 Cross on Cross

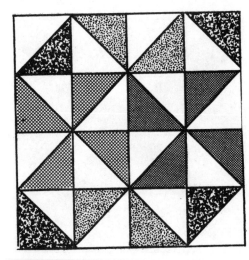

528 Old Windmill

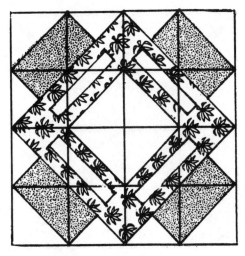

529 Children of Israel

530 Ozark Trail

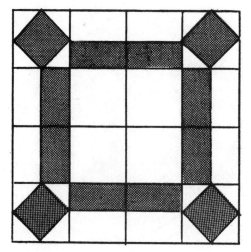

531 Johnnie Around the Corner

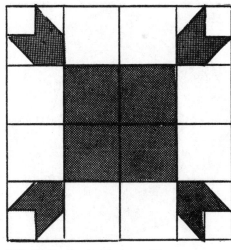

532 Tulip Lady Fingers II

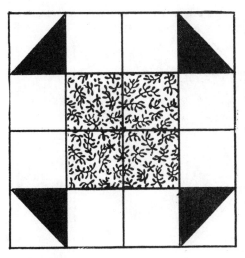

533 Puss in the Corner III

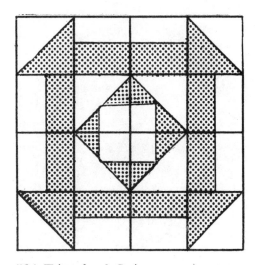

534 Triangles & Stripe

535 I Do

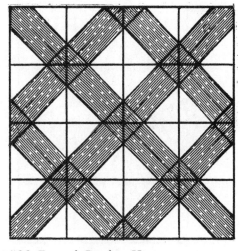

536 Formal Garden II

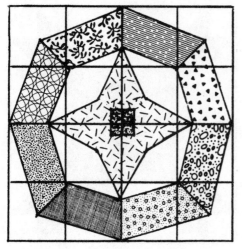

537 Star & Crown

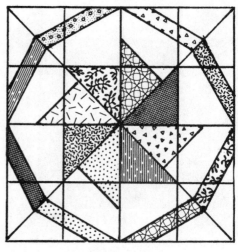

538 Wheel of Fortune I

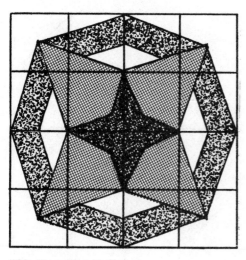

539 Drucilla's Delight

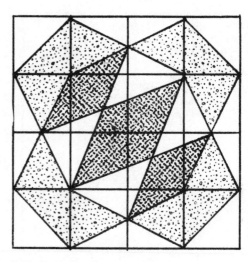

540 Dove in the Window

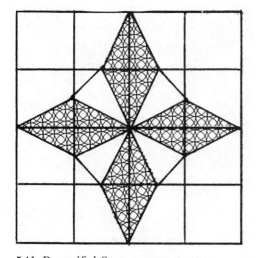

541 Beautiful Star

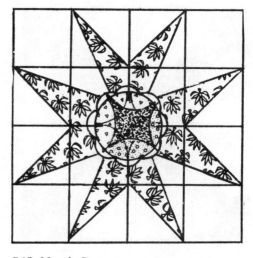

542 North Star

114

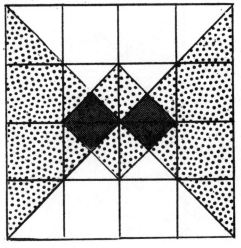

543 Granny's Choice

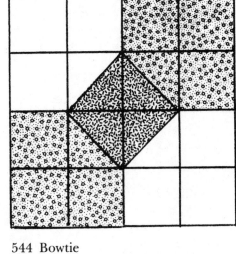

544 Bowtie

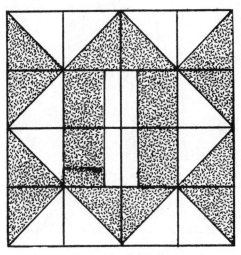

545 Broken Path

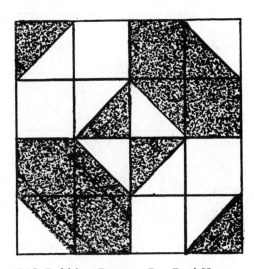

546 Robbing Peter to Pay Paul II

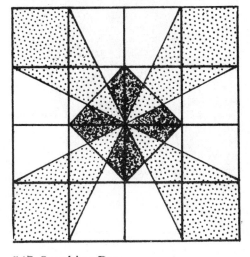

547 Sunshiny Day

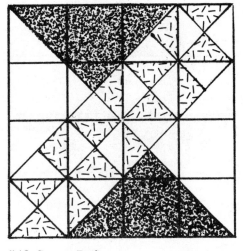

548 Starry Path

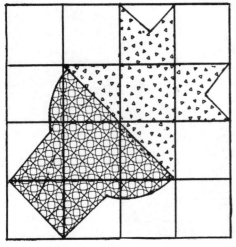

549 Calico Bouquet

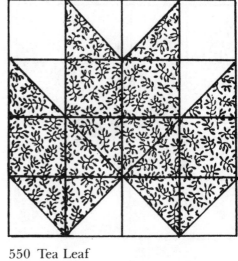

550 Tea Leaf

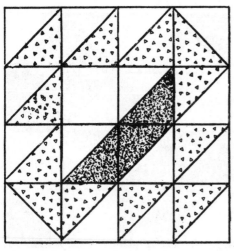

551 Little Lost Sailboat

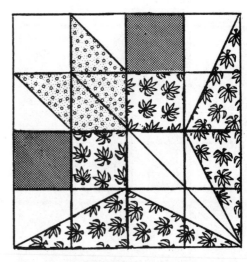

552 Crazy Quilt Flower

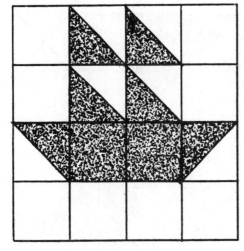

553 Ship

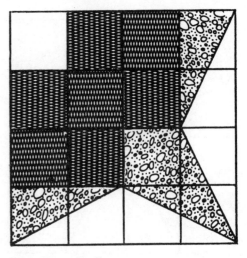

554 Crazy Quilt

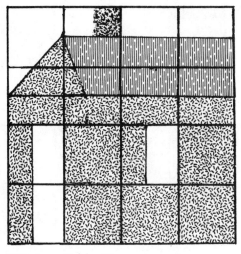

555 Log Cabin II

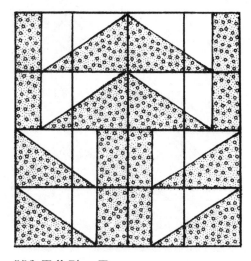

556 Tall Pine Tree

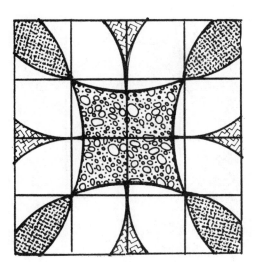

557 Rainbow Block

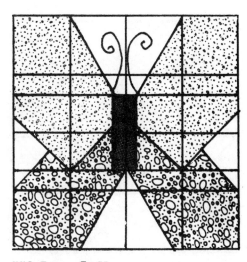

558 Butterfly II

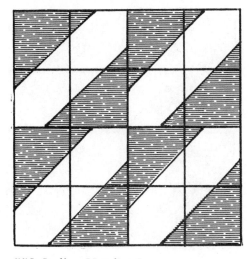

559 Indian Hatchet I

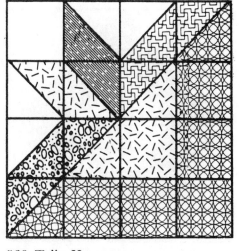

560 Tulip II

117

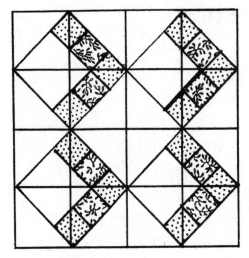

561 4-Patch Chain

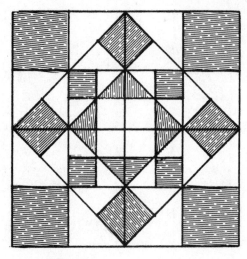

562 Hull's Victory

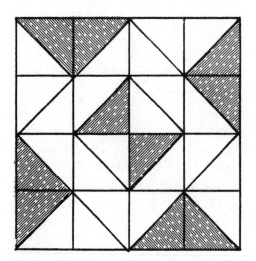

563 Blockade

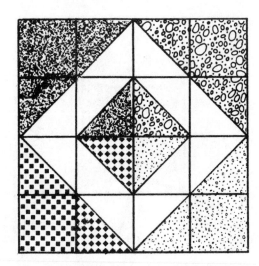

564 Friendship

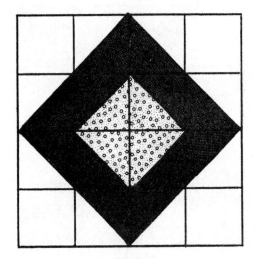

565 Friday the 13th

566 Rail Fence IV

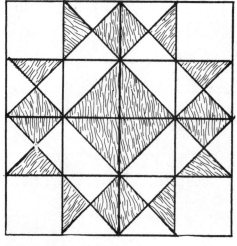
567 Beacon Lights

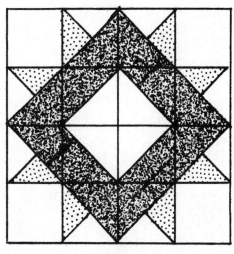
568 Noon & Light

569 Laurel Wreath

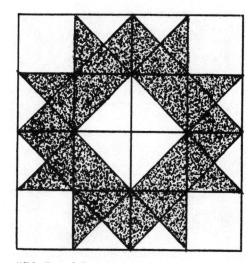
570 Royal Star

571 Country Path

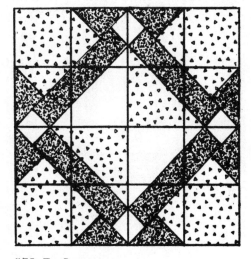
572 Ft. Sumter

573 Tea Rose

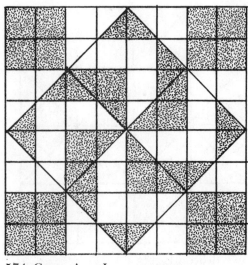

574 Crazy Ann I

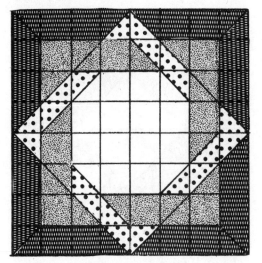

575 Interlocking Squares

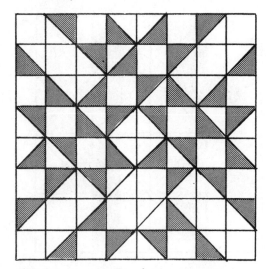

576 Interwoven Puzzle

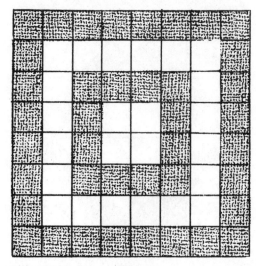

577 White House Steps

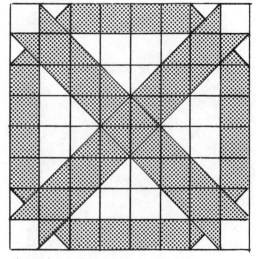

578 Three Crosses

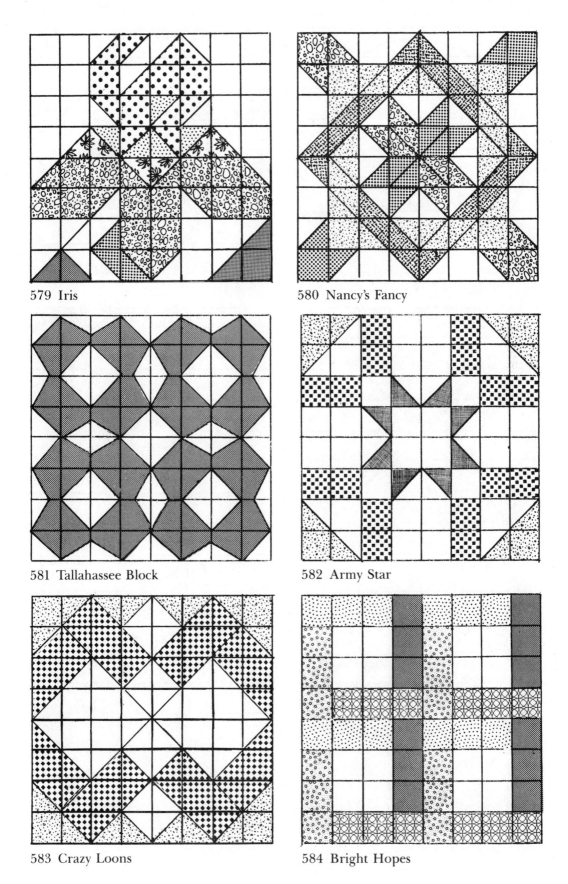

579 Iris

580 Nancy's Fancy

581 Tallahassee Block

582 Army Star

583 Crazy Loons

584 Bright Hopes

121

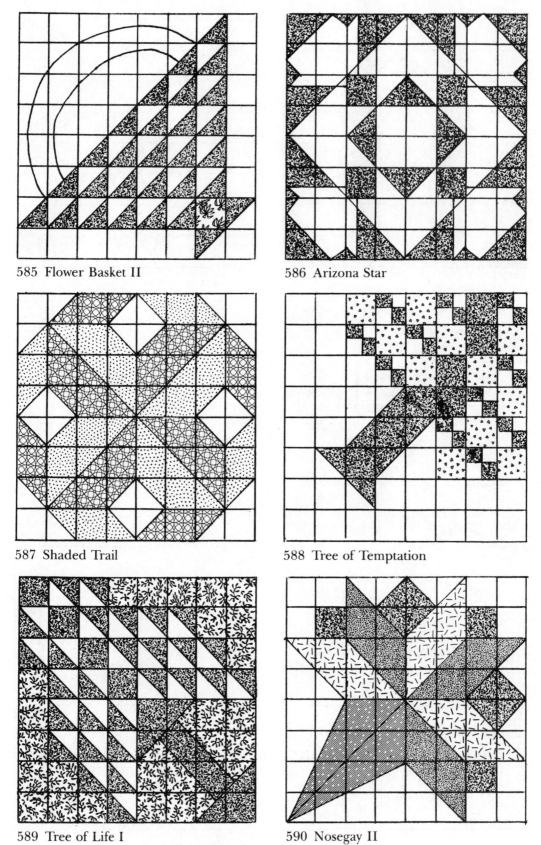

585 Flower Basket II

586 Arizona Star

587 Shaded Trail

588 Tree of Temptation

589 Tree of Life I

590 Nosegay II

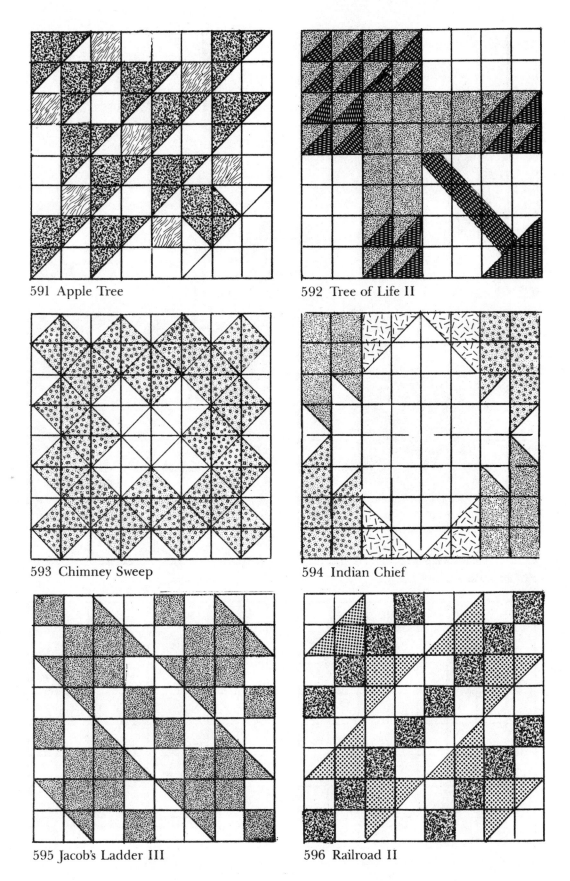

591 Apple Tree

592 Tree of Life II

593 Chimney Sweep

594 Indian Chief

595 Jacob's Ladder III

596 Railroad II

597 Georgetown Circles

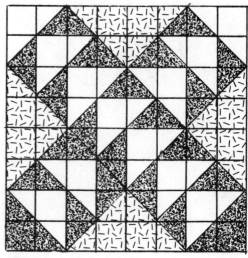

598 Railroad Crossing I

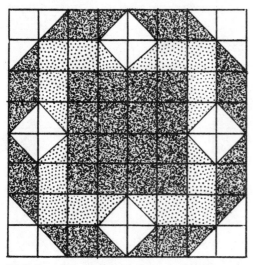

599 Providence Block I

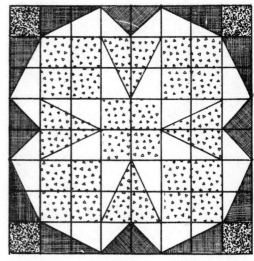

600 Eddystone Light

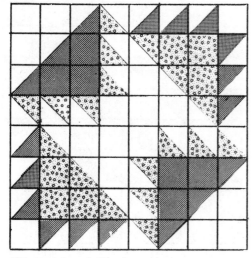

601 Barrister's Block

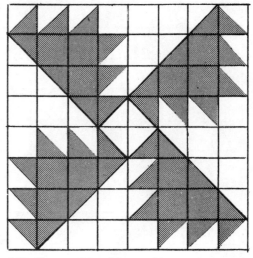

602 Kansas Troubles

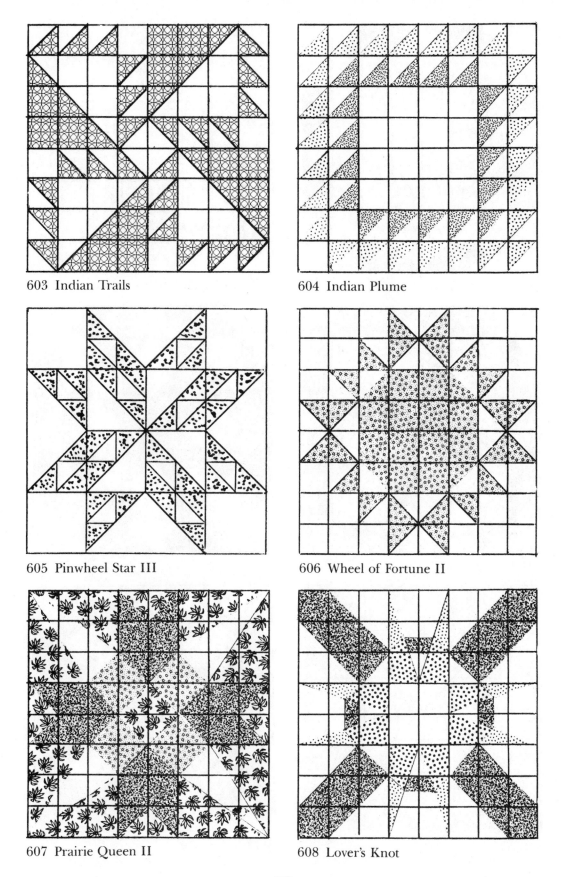

603 Indian Trails

604 Indian Plume

605 Pinwheel Star III

606 Wheel of Fortune II

607 Prairie Queen II

608 Lover's Knot

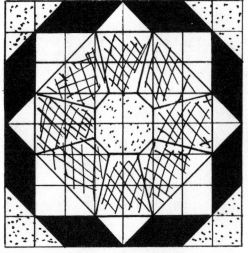

609 Diamond Star

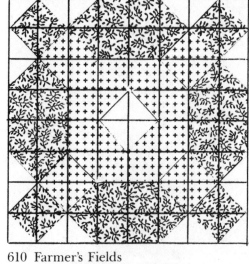

610 Farmer's Fields

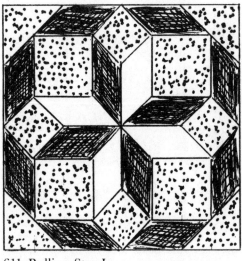

611 Rolling Star I

612 Star & Chains

613 Alaska

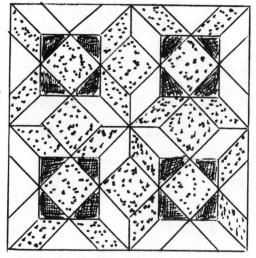

614 Harbor View

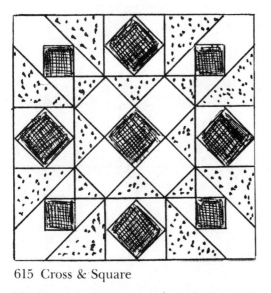

615 Cross & Square

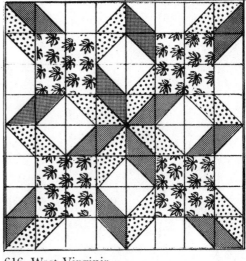

616 West Virginia

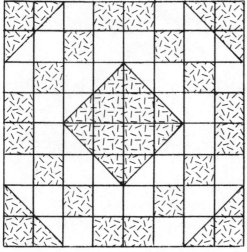

617 Jewel Box

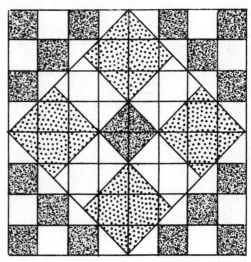

618 Pride of Ohio

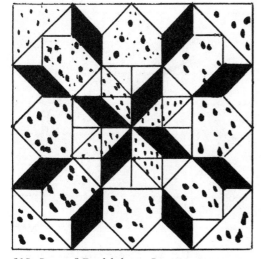

619 Star of Bethlehem I

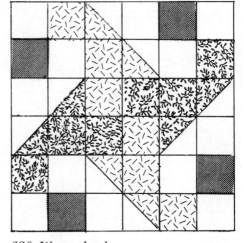

620 Waterwheel

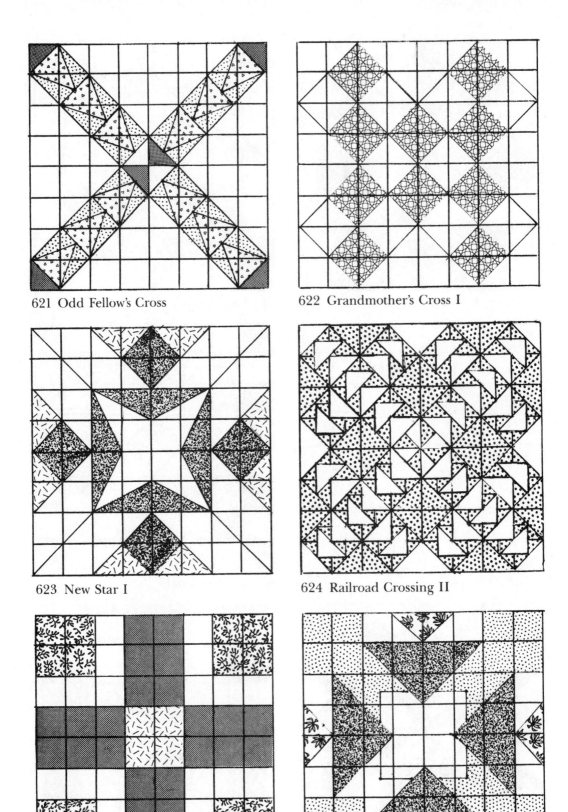

621 Odd Fellow's Cross

622 Grandmother's Cross I

623 New Star I

624 Railroad Crossing II

625 Red Cross III

626 Crow's Foot I

627 Little Giant

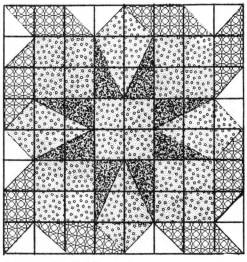

628 Springfield

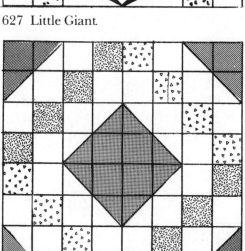

629 Irish Chain

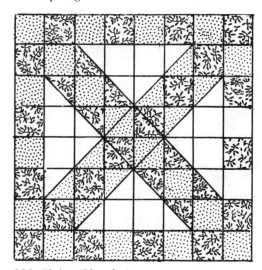

630 Flying Clouds I

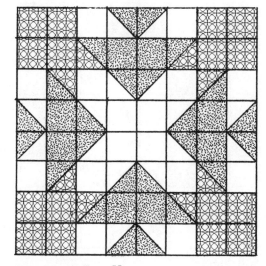

631 Crow's Foot II

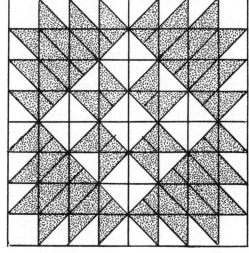

632 Delectable Mountains

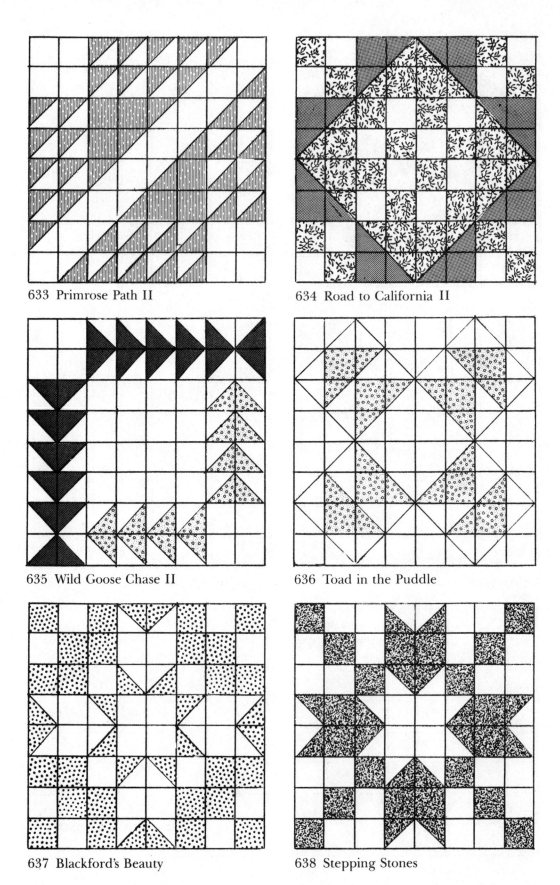

633 Primrose Path II

634 Road to California II

635 Wild Goose Chase II

636 Toad in the Puddle

637 Blackford's Beauty

638 Stepping Stones

130

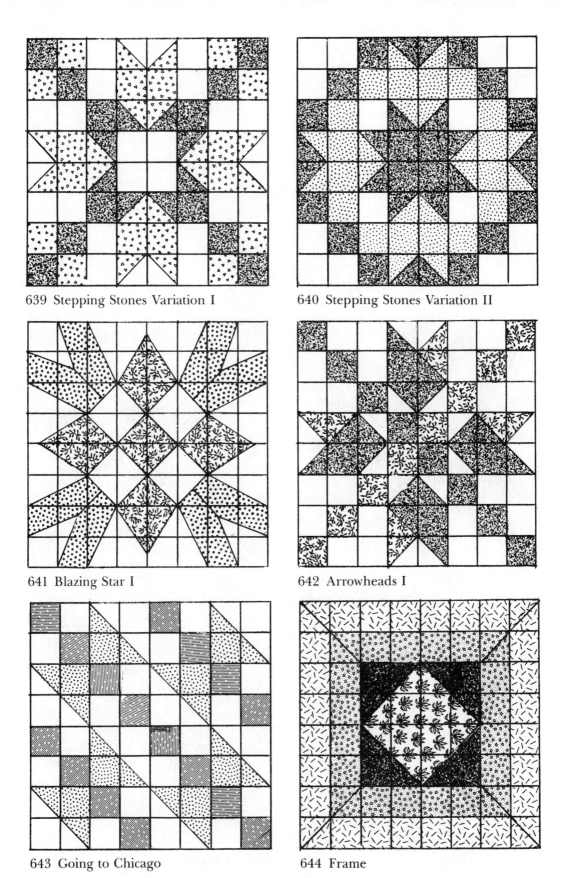

639 Stepping Stones Variation I

640 Stepping Stones Variation II

641 Blazing Star I

642 Arrowheads I

643 Going to Chicago

644 Frame

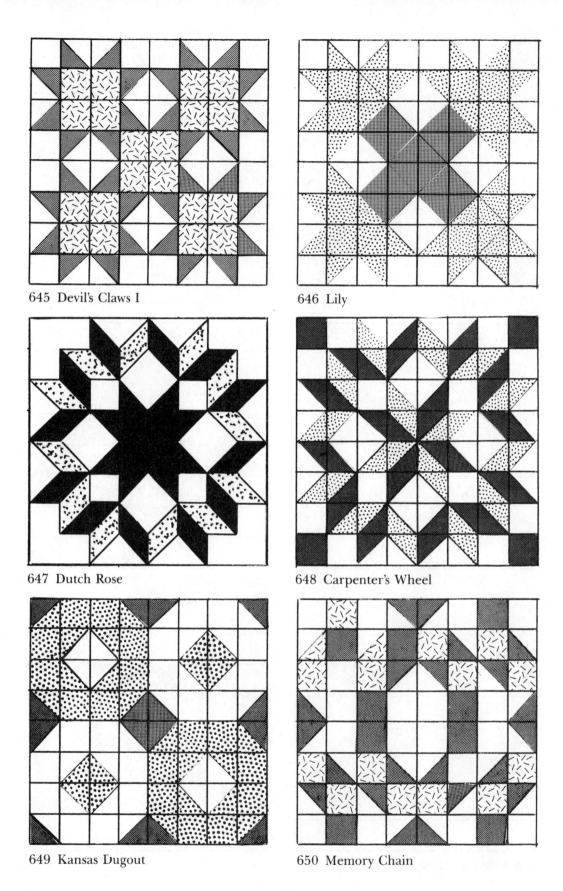

645 Devil's Claws I

646 Lily

647 Dutch Rose

648 Carpenter's Wheel

649 Kansas Dugout

650 Memory Chain

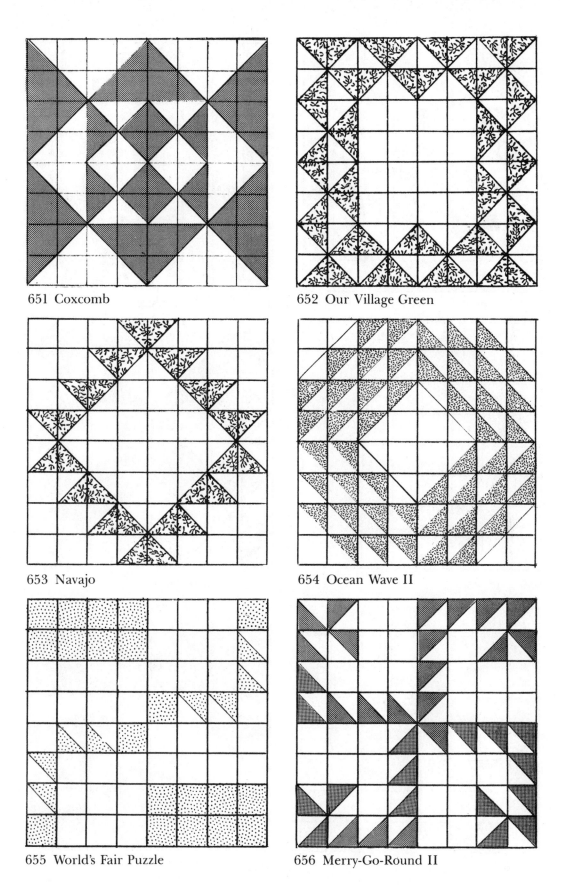

651 Coxcomb

652 Our Village Green

653 Navajo

654 Ocean Wave II

655 World's Fair Puzzle

656 Merry-Go-Round II

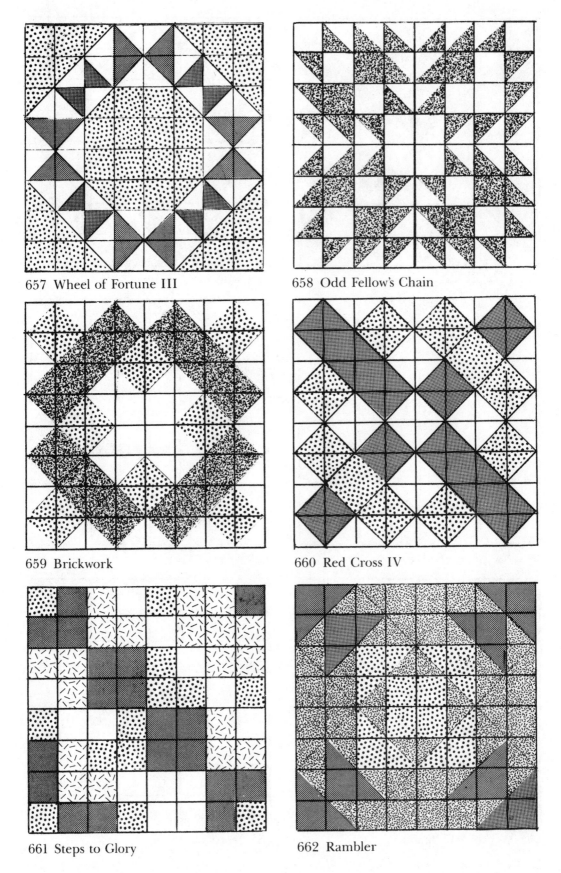

657 Wheel of Fortune III

658 Odd Fellow's Chain

659 Brickwork

660 Red Cross IV

661 Steps to Glory

662 Rambler

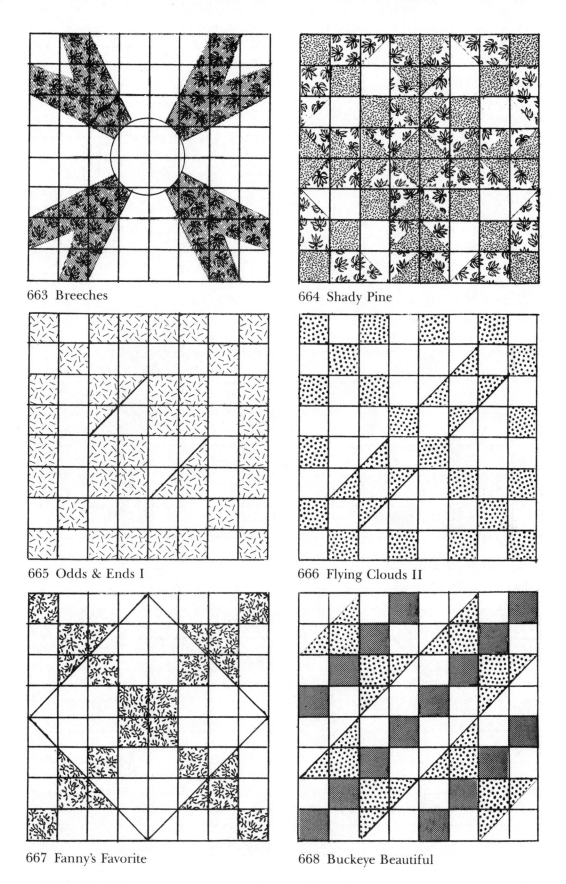

663 Breeches

664 Shady Pine

665 Odds & Ends I

666 Flying Clouds II

667 Fanny's Favorite

668 Buckeye Beautiful

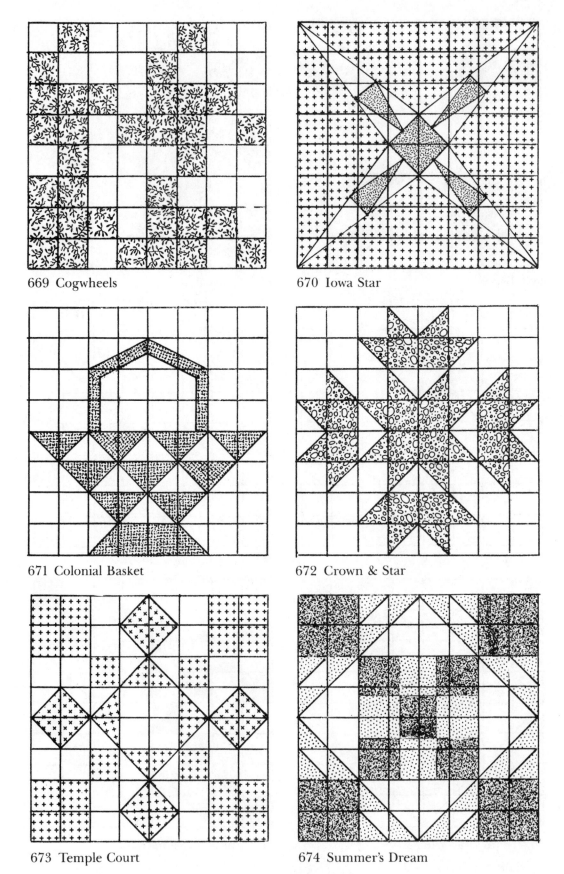

669 Cogwheels

670 Iowa Star

671 Colonial Basket

672 Crown & Star

673 Temple Court

674 Summer's Dream

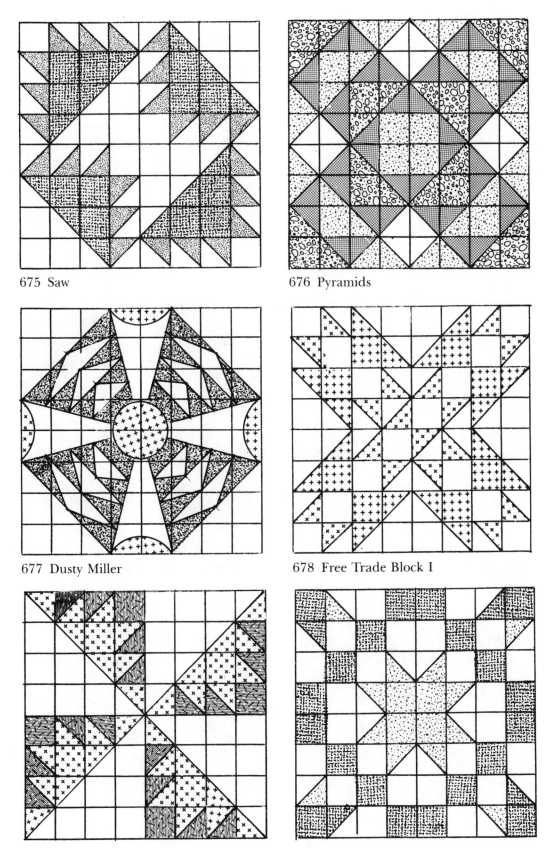

675 Saw

676 Pyramids

677 Dusty Miller

678 Free Trade Block I

679 Grand Right & Left

680 Kaleidoscope II

681 Sunny Lanes

682 Postage Stamp Basket

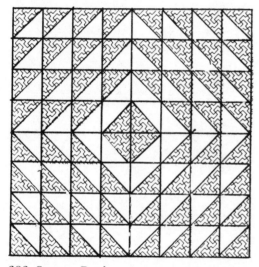

683 Square Deal

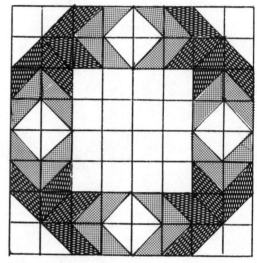

684 Cupid's Arrowpoint

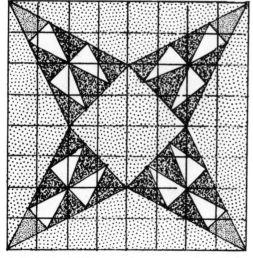

685 Lost Children

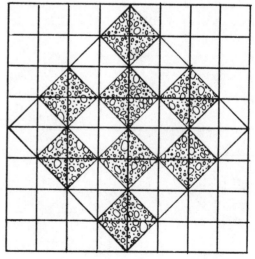

686 Coffin Star

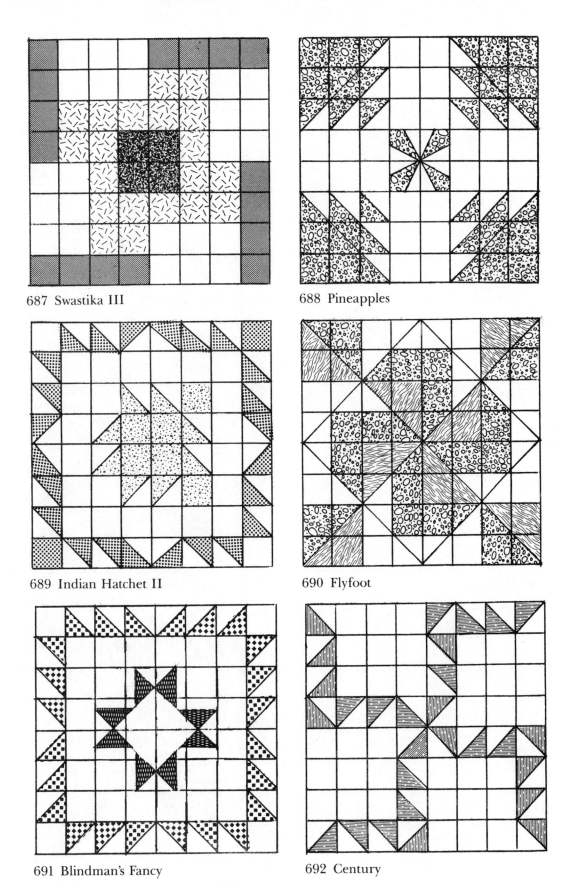

687 Swastika III

688 Pineapples

689 Indian Hatchet II

690 Flyfoot

691 Blindman's Fancy

692 Century

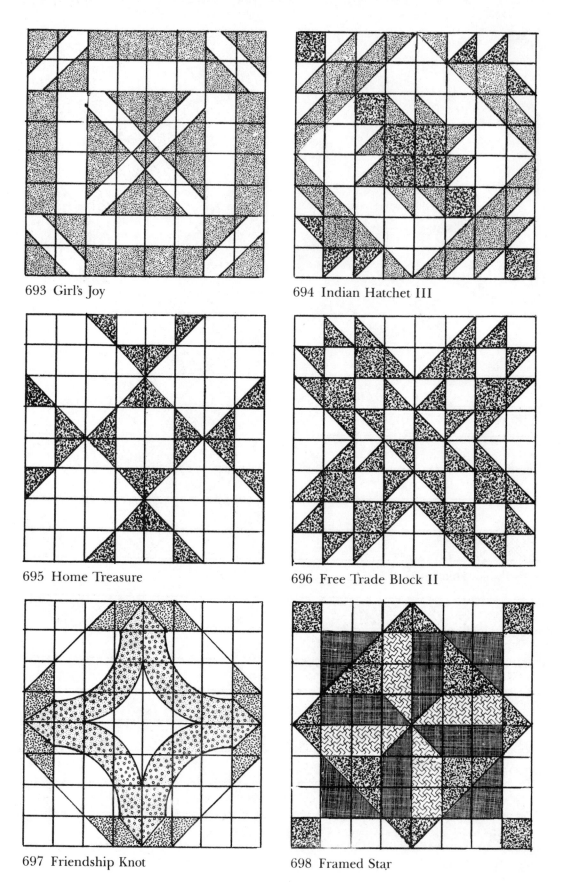

693 Girl's Joy

694 Indian Hatchet III

695 Home Treasure

696 Free Trade Block II

697 Friendship Knot

698 Framed Star

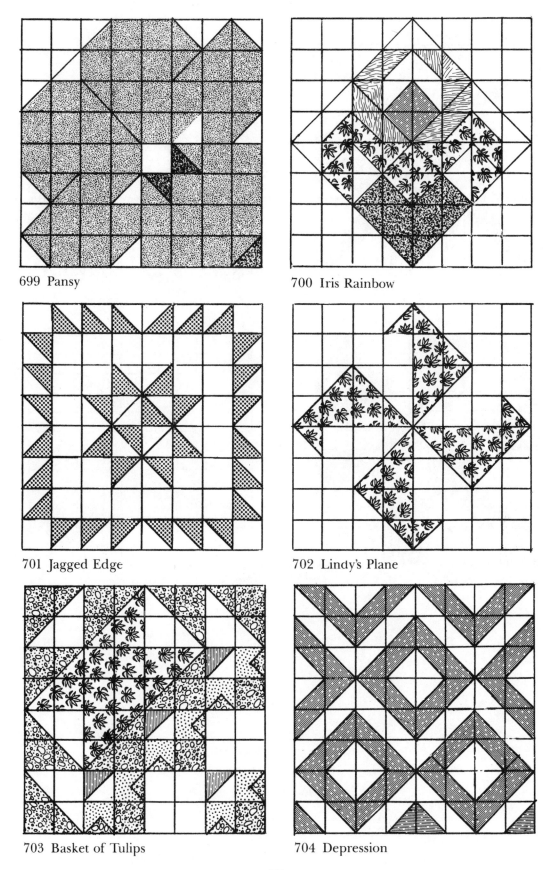

699 Pansy

700 Iris Rainbow

701 Jagged Edge

702 Lindy's Plane

703 Basket of Tulips

704 Depression

141

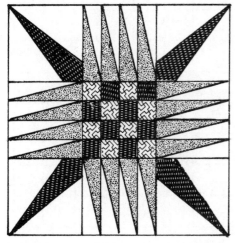

705 Thorny Thicket

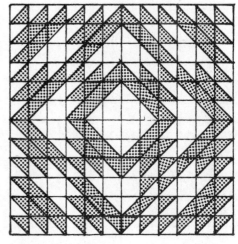

706 Sailboat

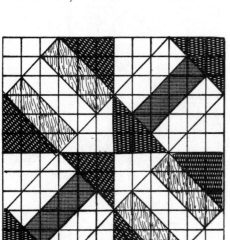

707 Chuck-a-Luck

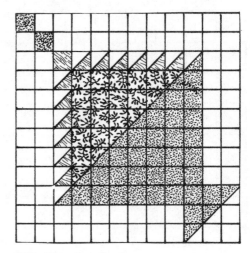

708 Hanging Basket

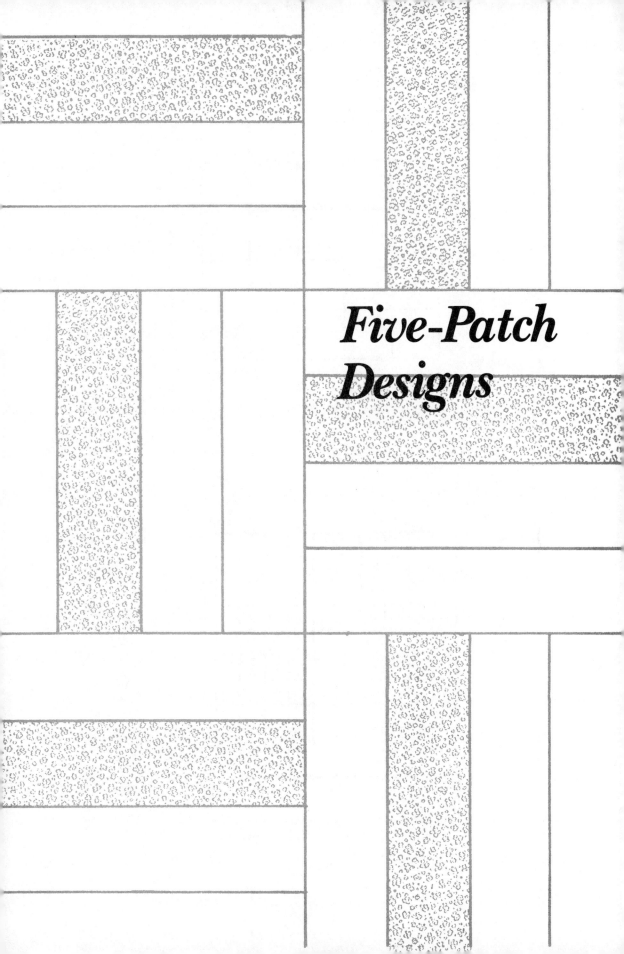

Five-Patch Designs

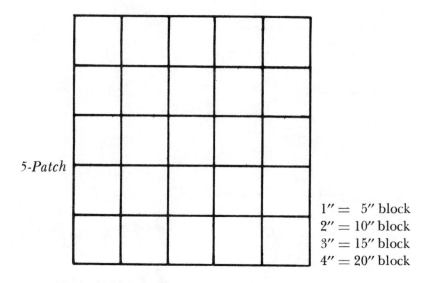

5-Patch

1″ = 5″ block
2″ = 10″ block
3″ = 15″ block
4″ = 20″ block

5-Patch—Each Square Divided in Half

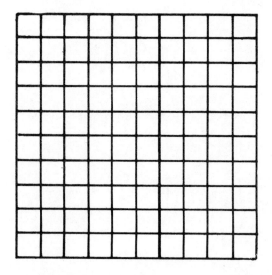

1″ = 10″ block
2″ = 20″ block

There are also a few 5-patch designs, divided into thirds, making a total of 15 squares across.

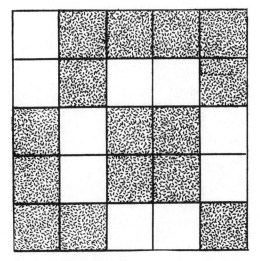

709 Children's Delight

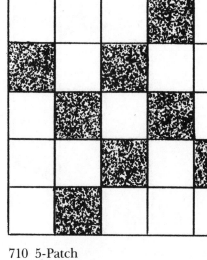

710 5-Patch

711 Plaid I

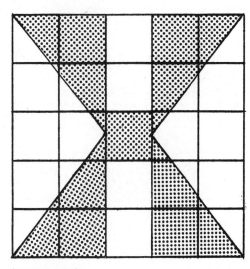

712 Bat Wing

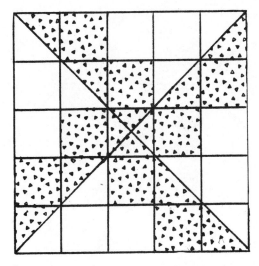

713 Broken Arrows I

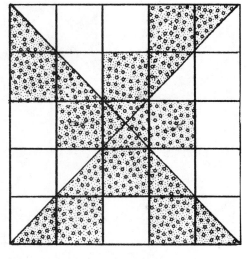

714 Broken Arrows II

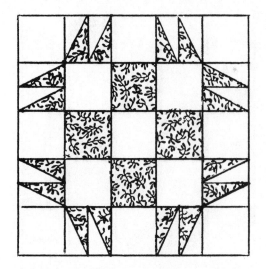

715 Pigeon Toes

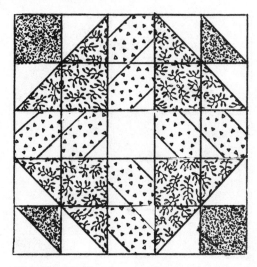

716 Mare's Nest

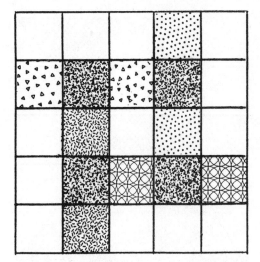

717 Flying Square

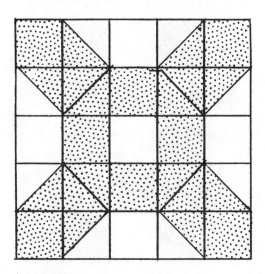

718 Domino

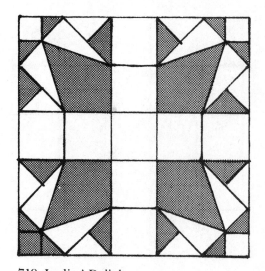

719 Ladies' Delight

720 Century of Progress II

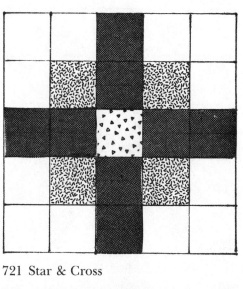

721 Star & Cross

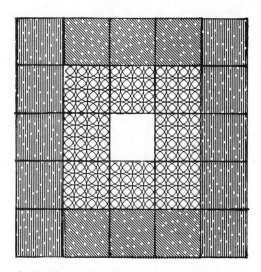

722 Blocks in a Box

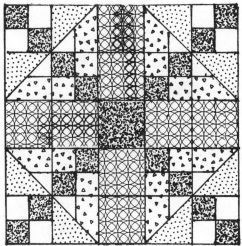

723 Easy Do

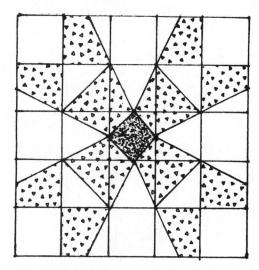

724 Dutch Mill

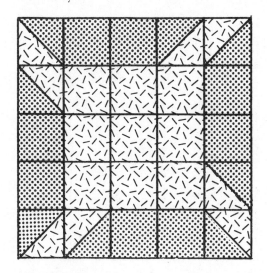

725 Captain's Wheel

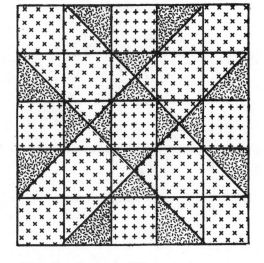

726 Handy Andy III

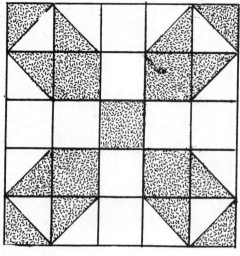

727 Fool's Square

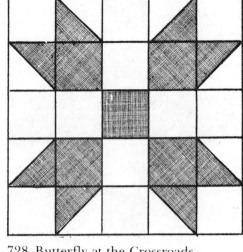

728 Butterfly at the Crossroads

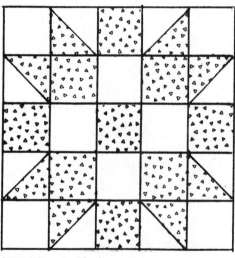

729 Sister's Choice

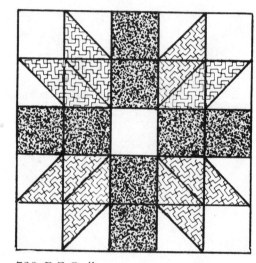

730 E-Z Quilt

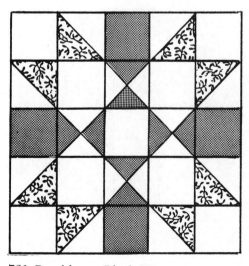

731 Providence Block II

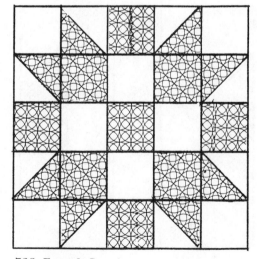

732 Four & Star

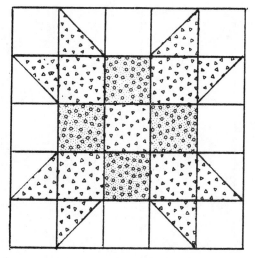

733 Farmer's Daughter

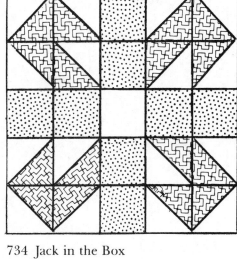

734 Jack in the Box

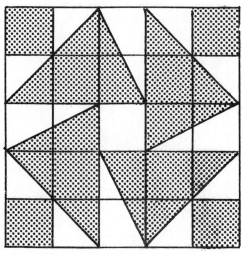

735 Follow the Leader

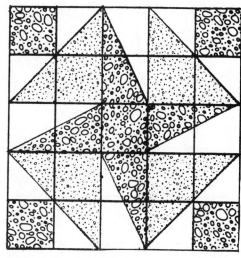

736 Crazy Ann II

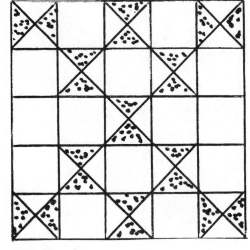

737 Clown

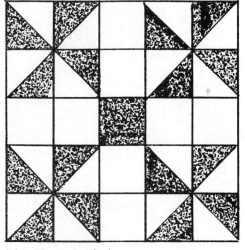

738 Honey's Choice

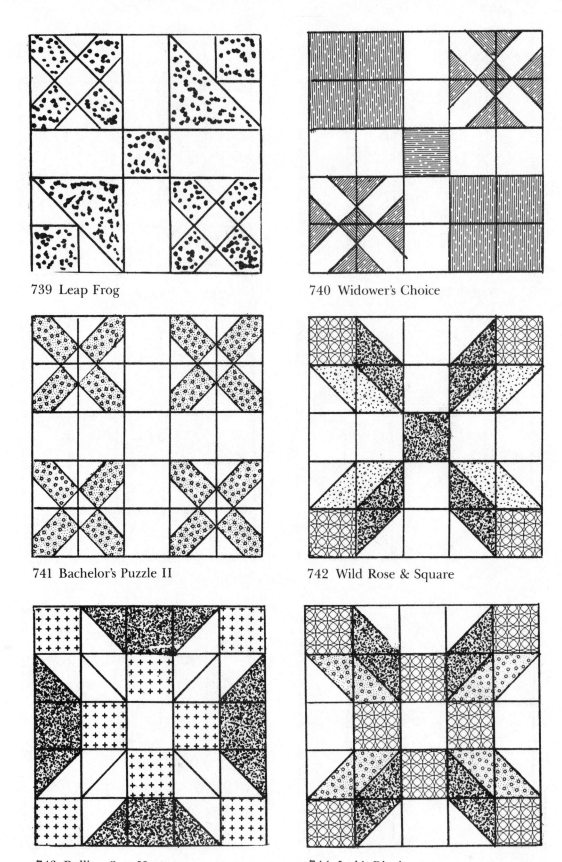

739 Leap Frog

740 Widower's Choice

741 Bachelor's Puzzle II

742 Wild Rose & Square

743 Rolling Star II

744 Jack's Blocks

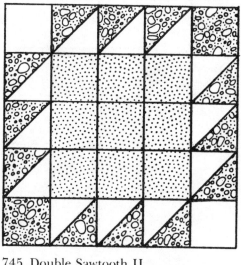

745 Double Sawtooth II

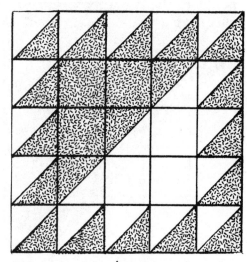

746 Lady of the Lake II

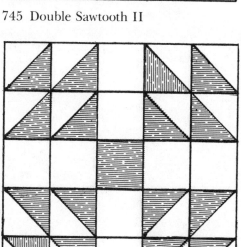

747 Flying Geese

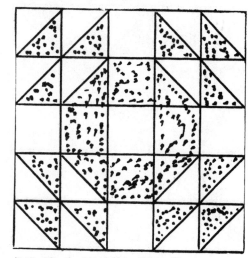

748 Single Wedding Ring II

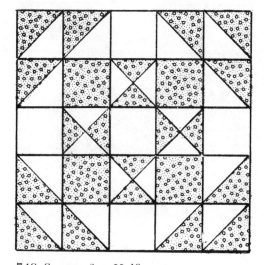

749 Square & a Half

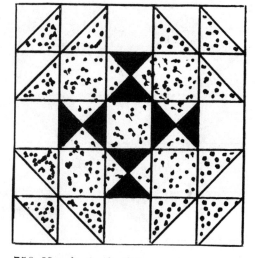

750 Handy Andy III

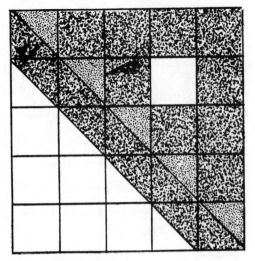

751 Greek Cross II

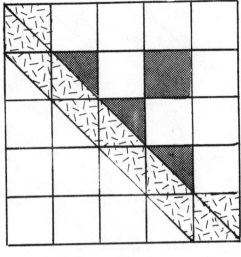

752 King's Crown II

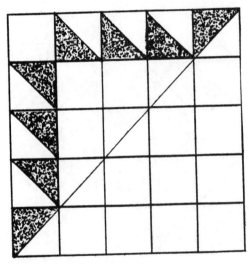

753 Star of Hope

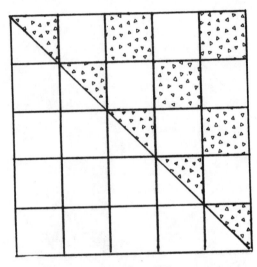

754 Steps to the Altar III

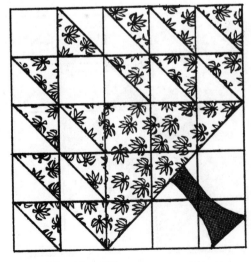

755 Pine Tree III

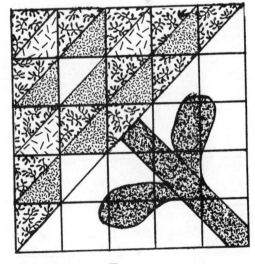

756 Christmas Tree

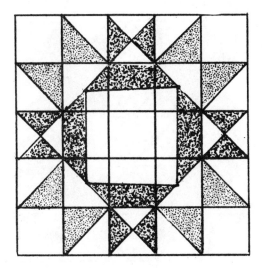

757 King David's Crown

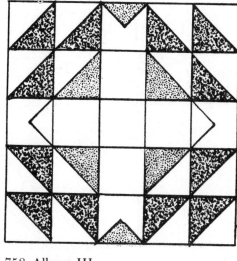

758 Album III

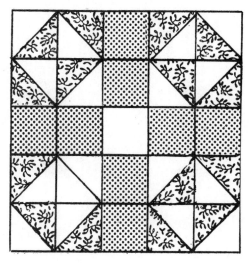

759 Red Cross V

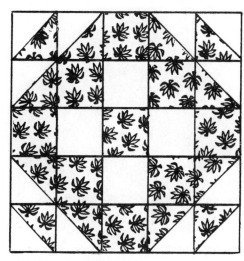

760 Duck & Ducklings I

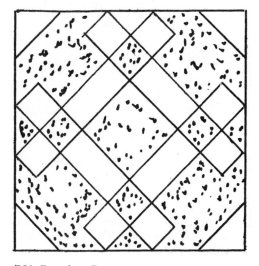

761 Domino Square

762 Ombre

153

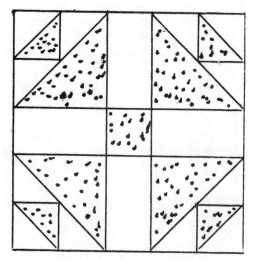

763 Duck & Ducklings II

764 Bird's Nest

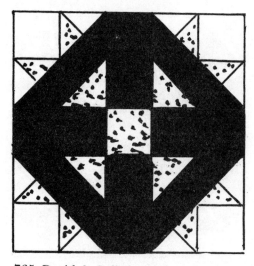

765 David & Goliath

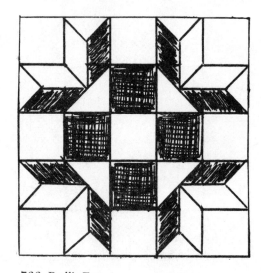

766 Bull's Eye

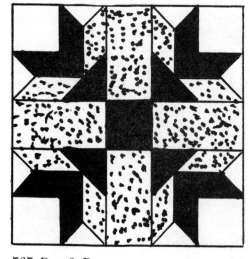

767 Doe & Darts

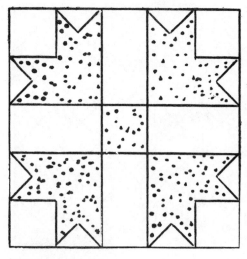

768 Cross & Crown

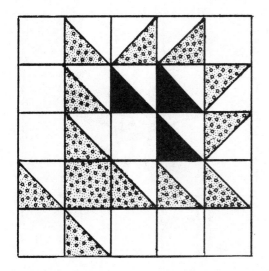

769 Fruit Basket

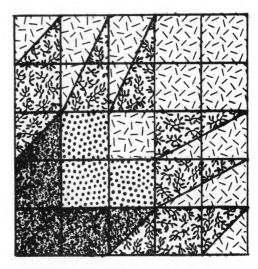

770 Southern Pine

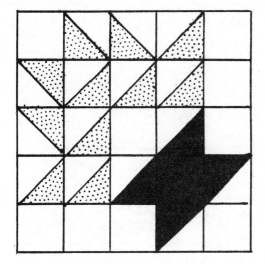

771 Grape Basket

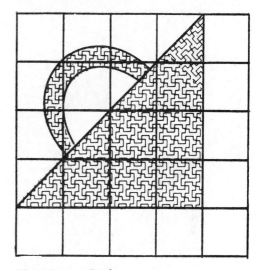

772 Flower Basket

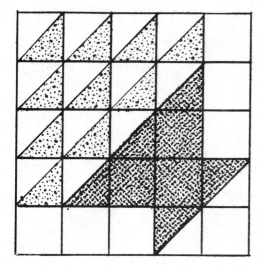

773 Flower Pot III

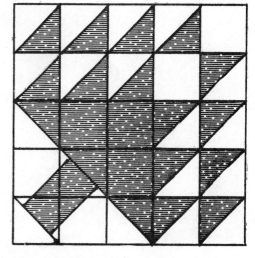

774 Pine Tree IV

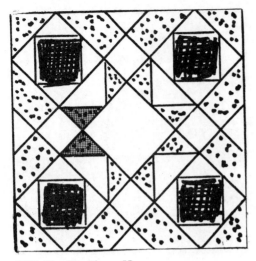

775 Devil's Claws II

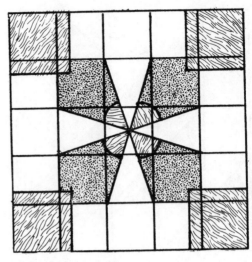

776 Four-Leaf Clover

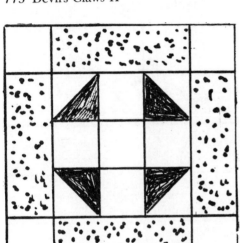

777 Philadelphia Pavement

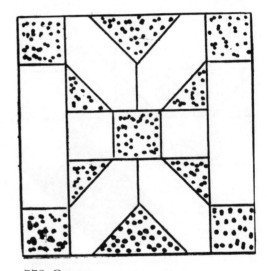

778 Oregon

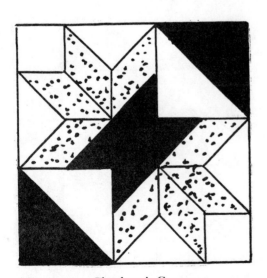

779 Queen Charlotte's Crown

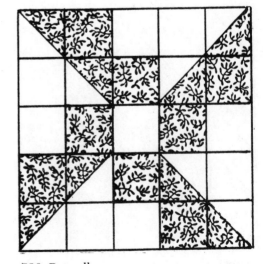

780 Propeller

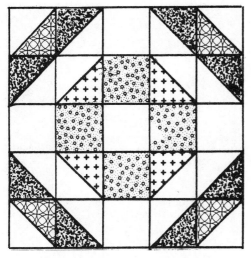

781 Wedding Rings

782 Mrs. Keller's 9-Patch

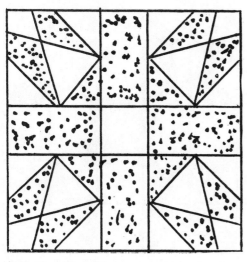

783 New Star II

784 Cross & Star

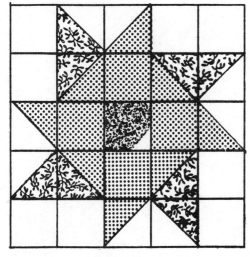

785 Hope of Hartford

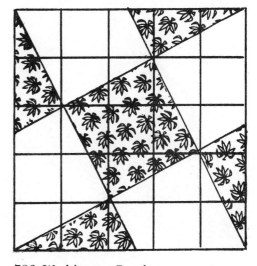

786 Washington Puzzle

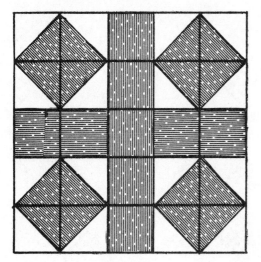

787 Garden of Eden

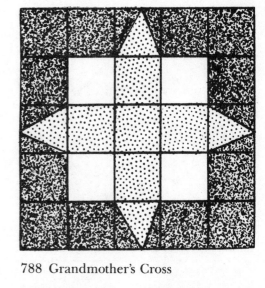

788 Grandmother's Cross

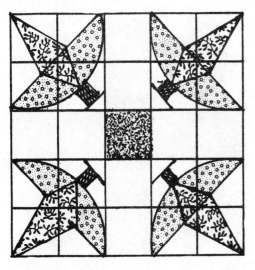

789 Swallows

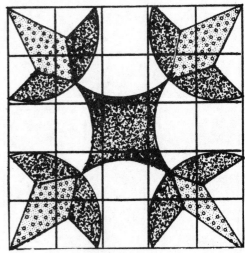

790 Turkey Tracks III

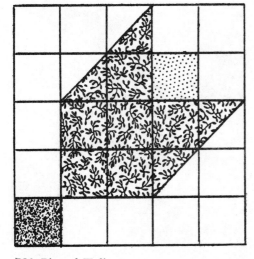

791 Pieced Tulip

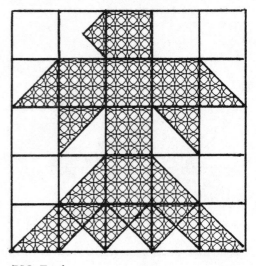

792 Eagle

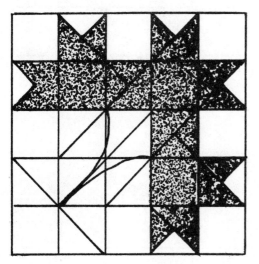

793 Cluster of Stars

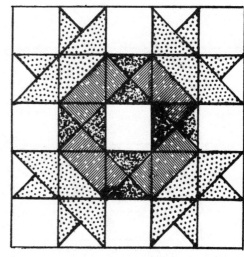

794 Golden Royalty

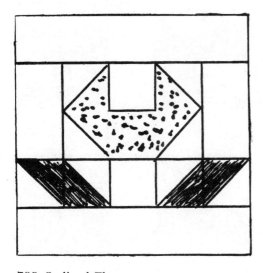

795 Stylized Flower

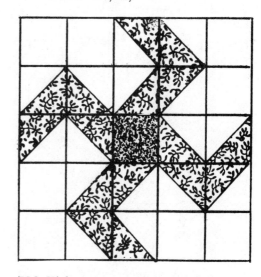

796 Kicks

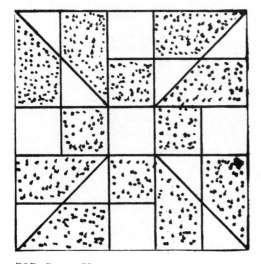

797 Crazy House

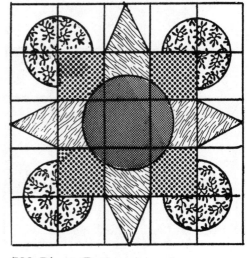

798 Disney Fantasy

159

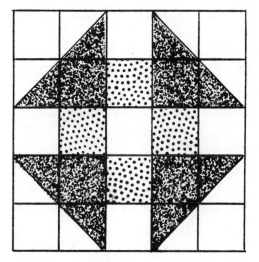

799 Churn Dash

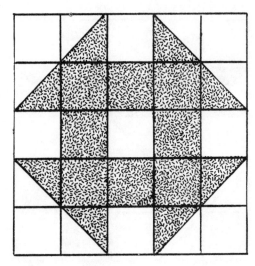

800 Double Wrench

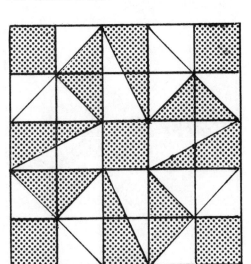

801 Pinwheel Square

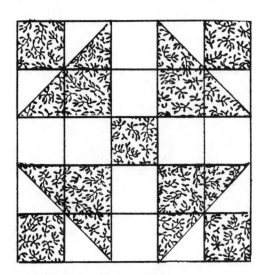

802 Grandmother's Choice I

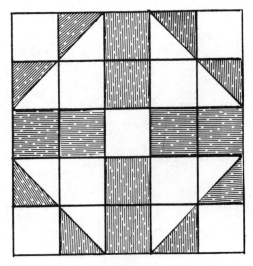

803 Grandmother's Choice II

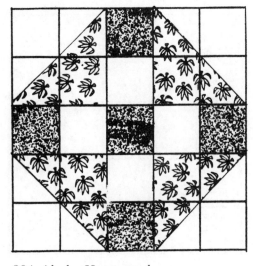

804 Alaska Homestead

805 Minnesota

806 Cousteau's Calypso

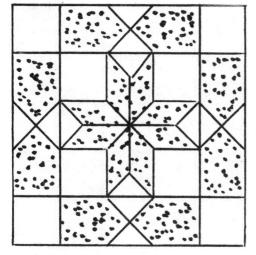

807 St. Louis Block

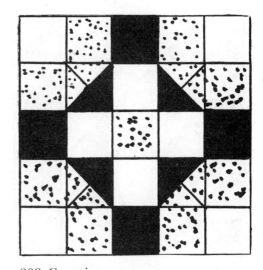

808 Georgia

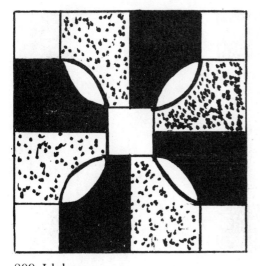

809 Idaho

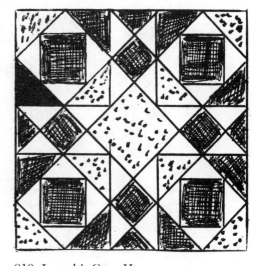

810 Joseph's Coat II

161

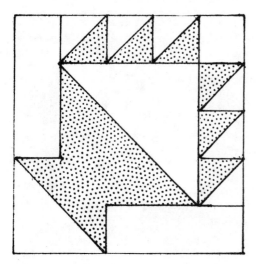

811 Cakestand

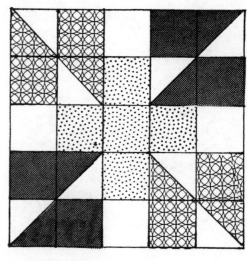

812 Z-Cross

813 Tent of Armageddon

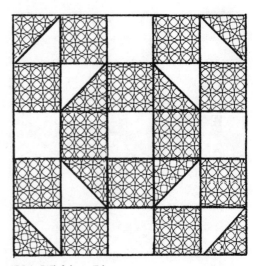

814 Wishing Ring

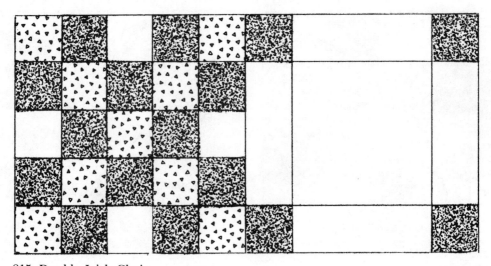

815 Double Irish Chain

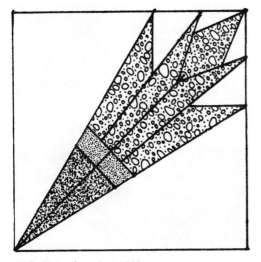

816 Shooting Star III

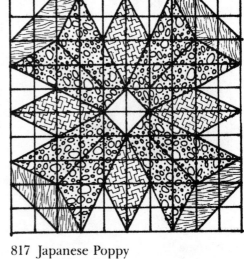

817 Japanese Poppy

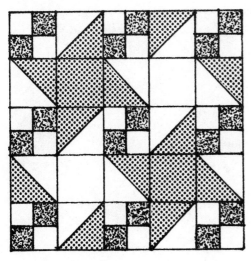

818 Milky Way I

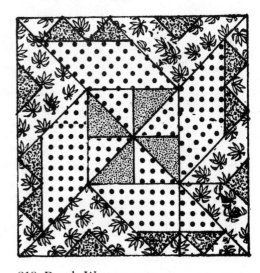

819 Dutch Waterways

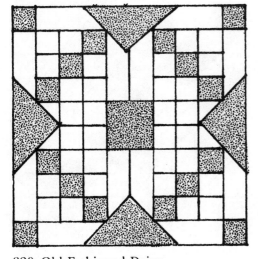

820 Old Fashioned Daisy

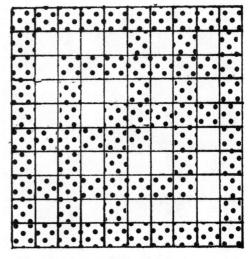

821 Carpenter's Square

163

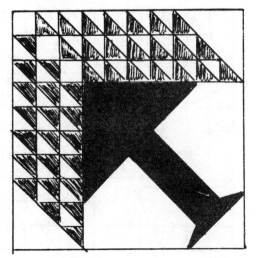

822 Pine Tree V

823 Linton

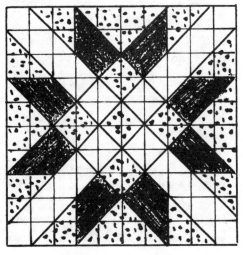

824 Mexican Cross

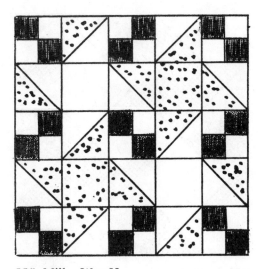

825 Milky Way II

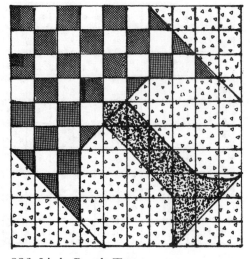

826 Little Beech Tree

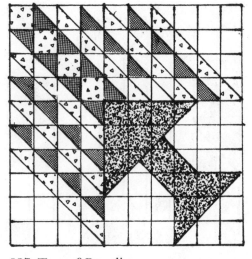

827 Tree of Paradise

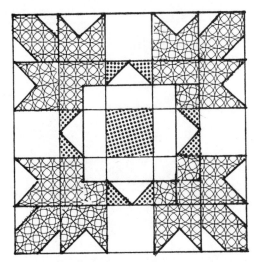

828 Autumn Leaves

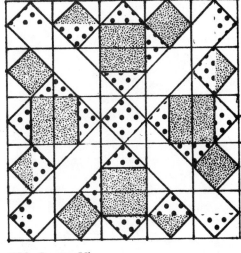

829 Grape Vine

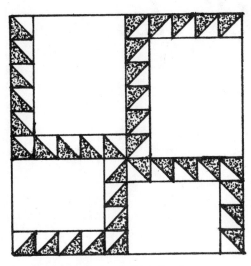

830 Grandmother's Pinwheel

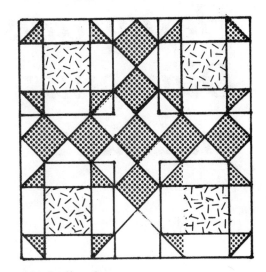

831 Indian Squares

832 Old Maid's Ramble

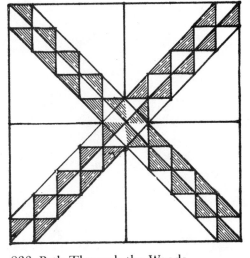

833 Path Through the Woods

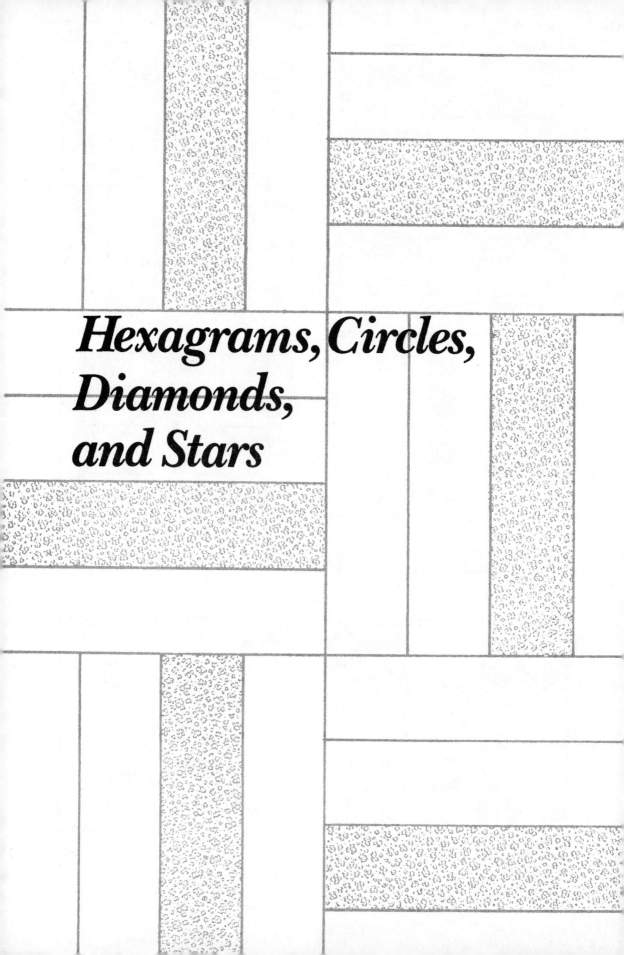

Hexagrams, Circles, Diamonds, and Stars

DRAFTING THE PATTERN

On a large sheet of paper draw a square the final size of the block. Rule it into the same number of squares as shown in the pattern. Draw in the lines in each square.

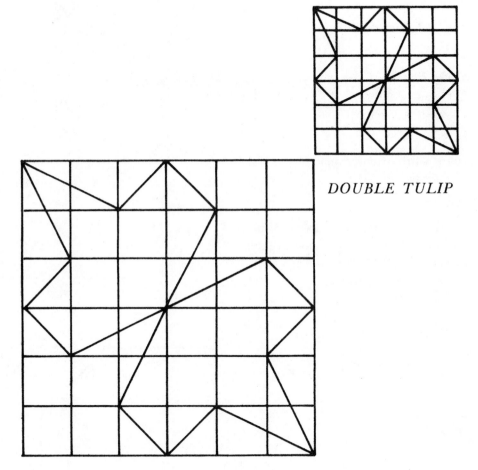

DOUBLE TULIP

CIRCLES

Circles can be drawn by using plates, saucers, cups, pan lids, and so forth, in the appropriate size. This seems a rather haphazard method, but I've never found the string and pencil method satisfactory, and I've yet to find a compass that will draw an 18″ circle.

The pattern pieces for designs such as Tobacco Leaf are made by laying the circle template's edge at the corner of the square. Position it so that it crosses the corner of the center square. Trace around the template. Repeat for the other edge of the elliptical shape.

DRAFTING AN 8-POINT STAR

Trace octagon onto full-size block. Lay a ruler along edges and enlarge to proper size.

Draw in guidelines as shown.

Find length of this line to center.

From center, measure along center lines outward the same distance as the arrow line. Mark with a dot.

Draw a line from corner to dot. Your diamond is complete.

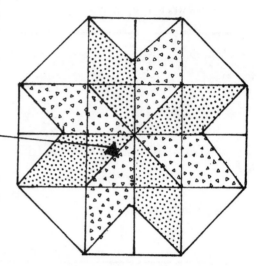

There are plastic templates available for both 45° and 60° diamond shapes, as well as for hexagons, but it's always nice to be able to draft the shape to fit your block exactly.

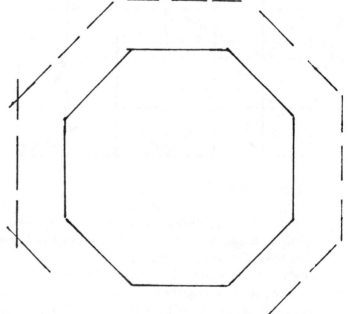

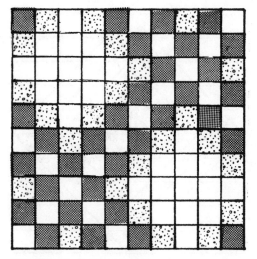

834 Triple Irish Chain

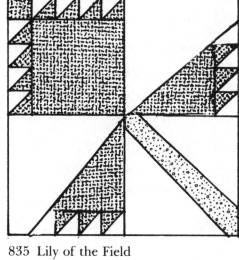

835 Lily of the Field

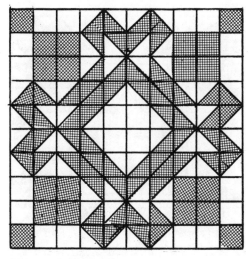

836 Cathedral Window

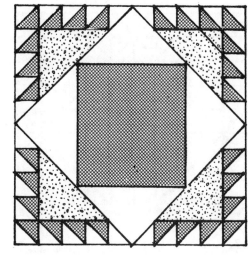

837 Pine Burr I

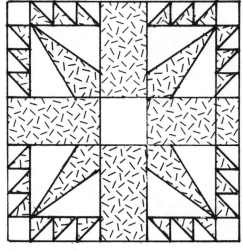

838 Odd Star

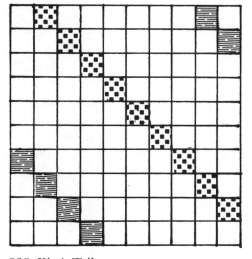

839 Kite's Tail

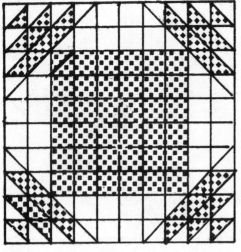

840 Pine Burr II

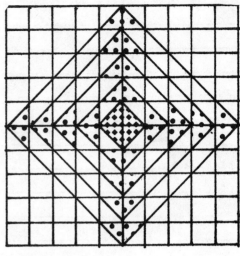

841 Church Steps

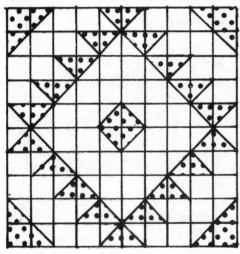

842 Zig Zag

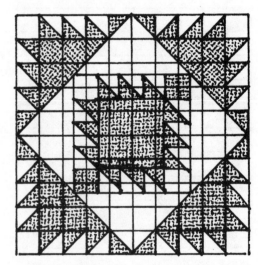

843 Solomon's Temple

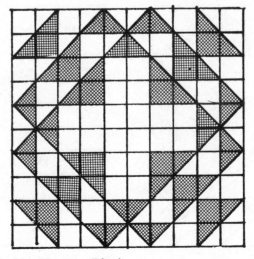

844 Memory Block

170

6-POINT STAR

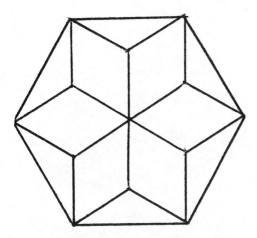

The 6-point star is based on a hexagon.

Enlarge the hexagon by laying a ruler along each edge and marking it up until it is the desired size for the block.

Draw in the guidelines as shown, beginning with the lines touching the outer edges, and ending with the center lines.

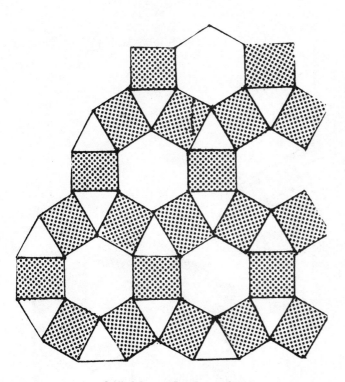

845 Merry-Go-Round III

846 Wedding Tile

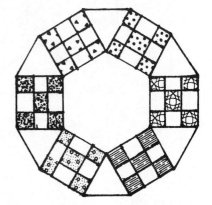

847 Jack's Chain

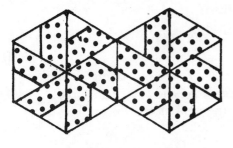

848 Whirligig III

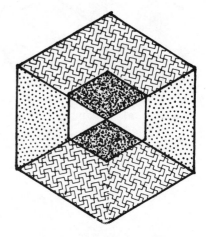

849 Spider Web IV

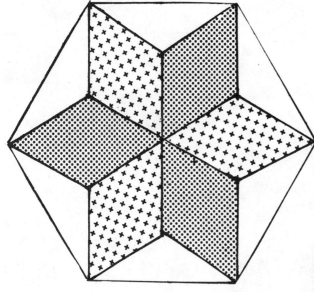

850 Eisenhower Star

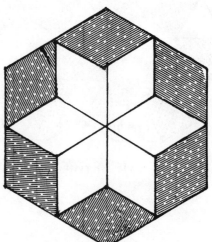

851 Tea Box

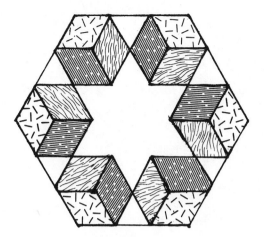

852 Columbia

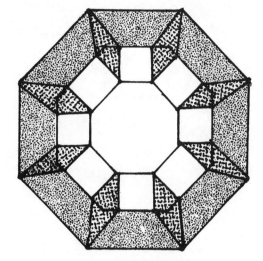

853 Castle Wall

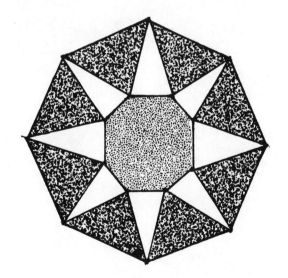

854 Rising Sun

855 Old Glory

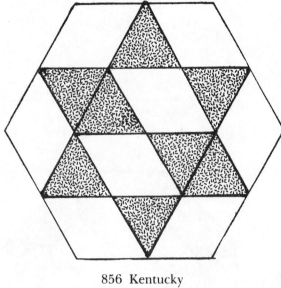

856 Kentucky

857 Octagon

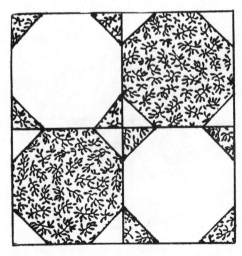

858 Robbing Peter to Pay Paul III

174

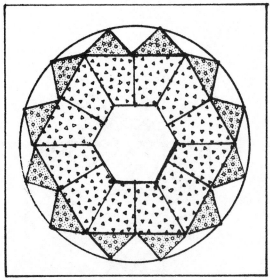

859 Queen of the May

860 Liberty Star

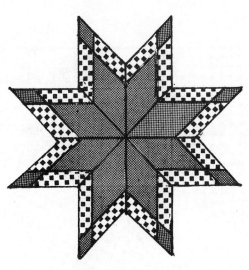

861 Virginia Star

862 Tennessee Star

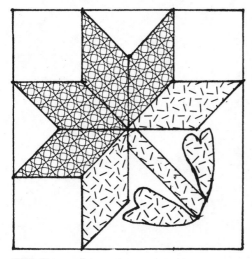

863 Peony I

864 Flying Swallows

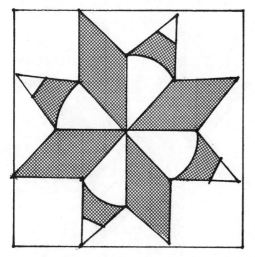

865 King's Crown III

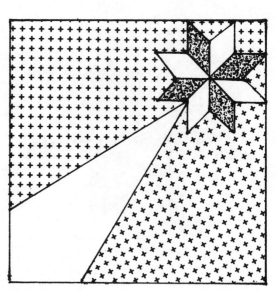

866 Missouri

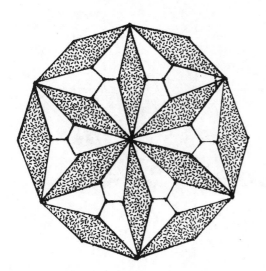

867 Chained Star

868 Star of LeMoyne

869 Aurora Borealis

870 Aunt Martha's Rose

871 Orange Peel II

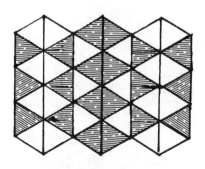

872 Skyscraper

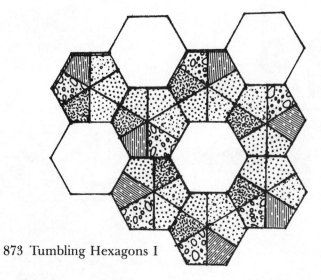

873 Tumbling Hexagons I

874 Ozark Diamonds

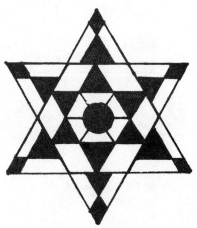

875 Colorado Star

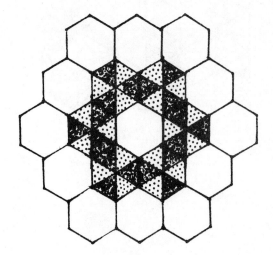

876 Snow Crystal

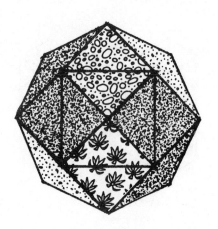

877 Jewel II

878 Silver & Gold

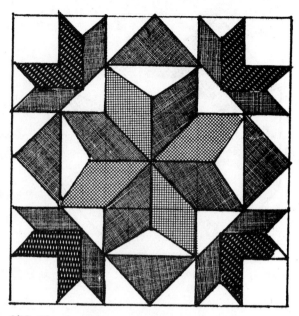

879 Pinwheel Star

880 . Lucinda's Star

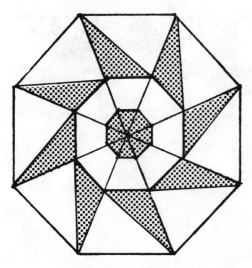

881 Flying Saucer

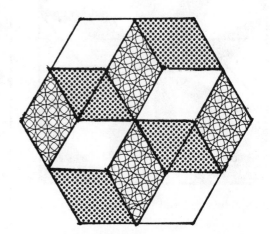

882 Block Puzzle I

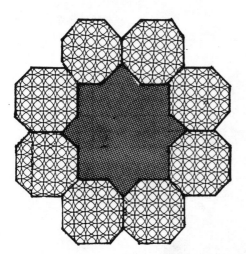

883 Old Staffordshire

884 8 Diamonds & a Star

885 Meadow Flower

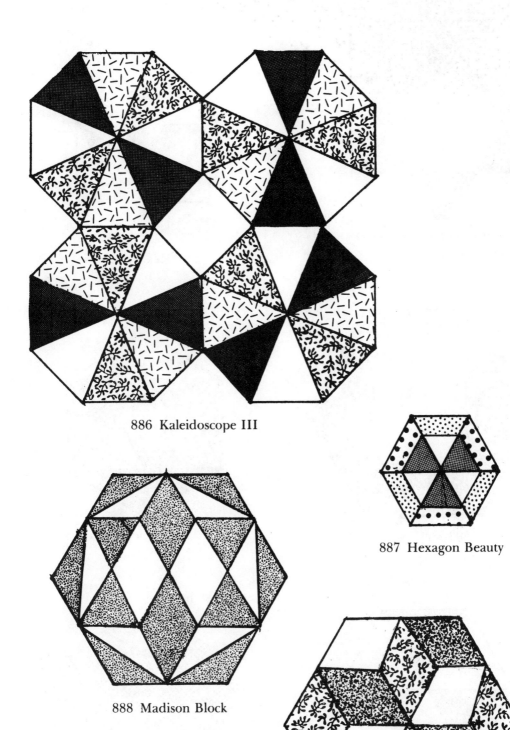

886 Kaleidoscope III

887 Hexagon Beauty

888 Madison Block

889 Block Puzzle II

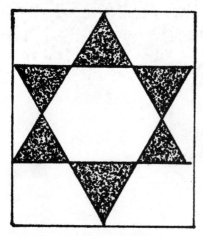

890 Star of Bethlehem II

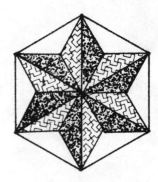

891 Hexagon Star

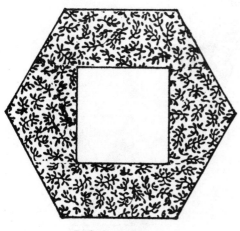

892 Stop Sign

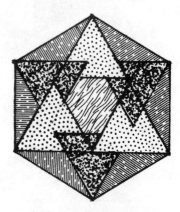

893 Interlocked Star

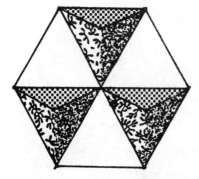

894 Wonder of Egypt

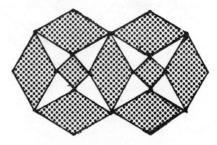

895 Diamond & Star

896 Cosmos

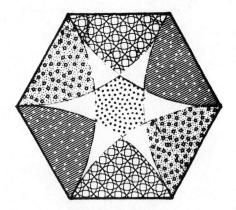

897 Star of the Mountains

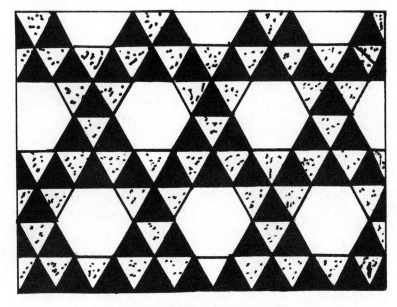

898 Tumbling Hexagons II

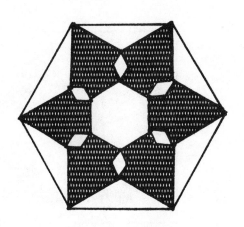

899 Arrowheads II

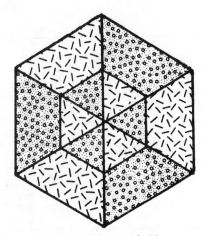

900 Spider Web V

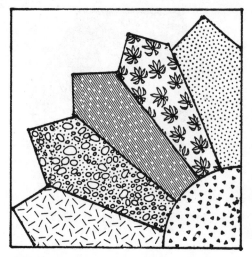

901 Mary's Fan

902 Four O'clock

903 Circle within Circle

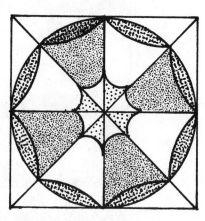

904 Electric Fan

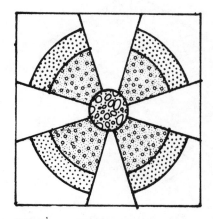

905 Texas Tulip

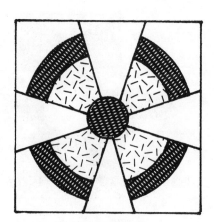

906 Air Ship Propeller

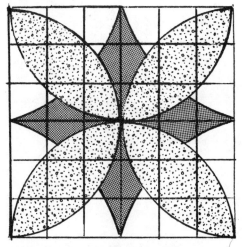

907 Alabama Beauty

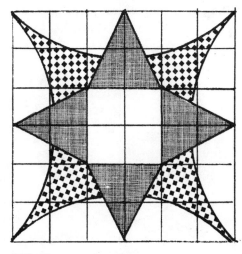

908 Homemaker

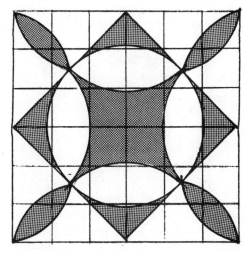

909 Indiana

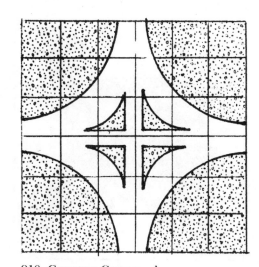

910 Country Crossroads

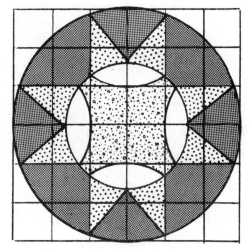

911 Caesar's Crown

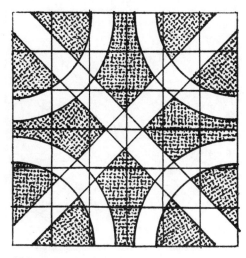

912 Crossroads

185

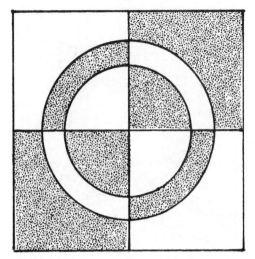

913 Fair Play

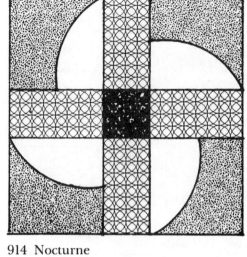

914 Nocturne

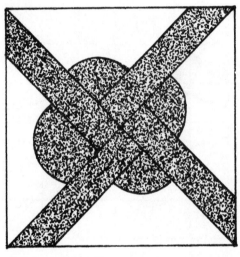

915 Josephine Knot

916 Hidden Flower

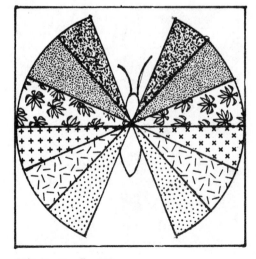

917 Butterfly III

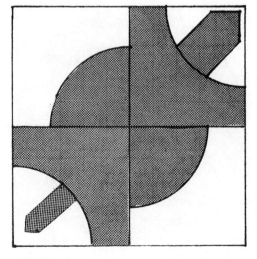

918 Turtle

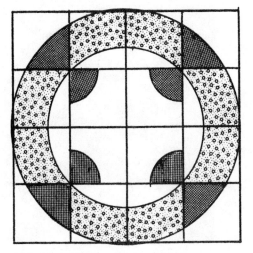

919 Queen's Crown I

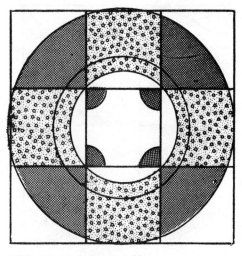

920 Queen's Crown II

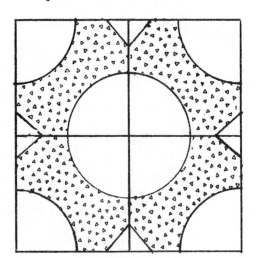

921 Pullman Puzzle I

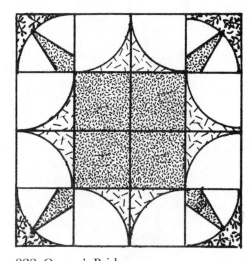

922 Queen's Pride

923 Compass I

924 Old Maid Combination

925 Millwheel

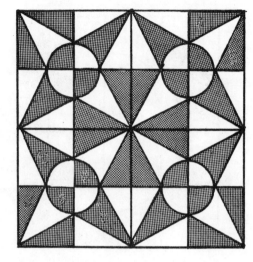

926 Compass II

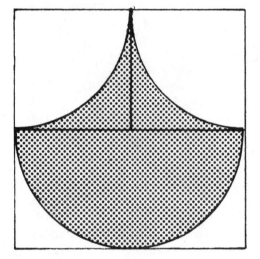

927 Shell

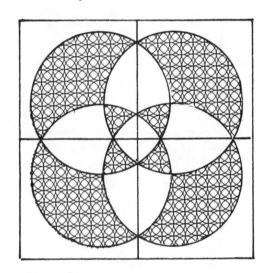

928 Utah

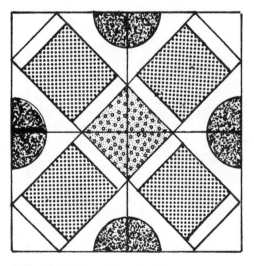

929 Old Missouri

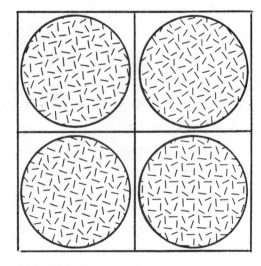

930 Ohio Beauty

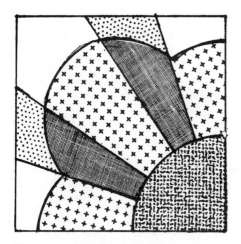

931 Grandmother's Fan I

932 Flo's Fan

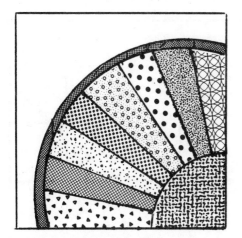

933 Grandmother's Fan II

934 Fan

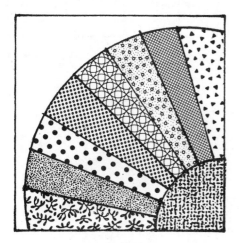

935 Patchwork Fan

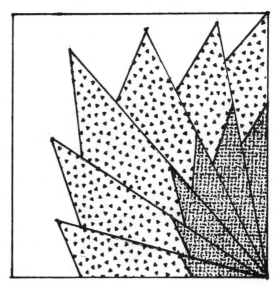

936 Milady's Fan

937 Snake in the Hollow

938 Dresden Plate

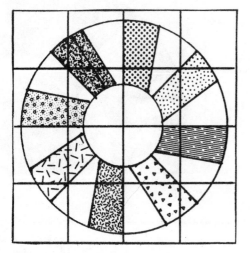

939 Circle of Life

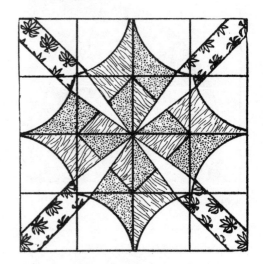

940 Grandmother's Choice IV

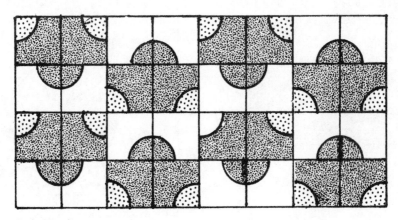

941 Mushrooms

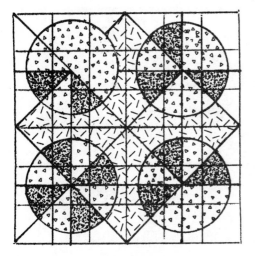

942 Moon & Stars

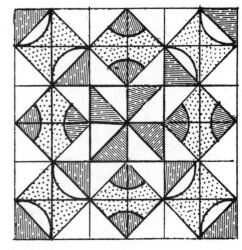

943 Arkansas II

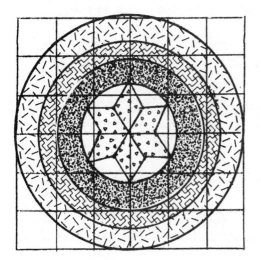

944 Rainbow Star

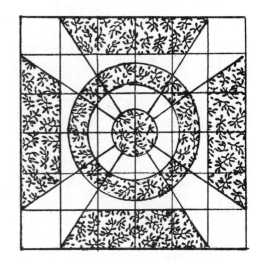

945 Nevada

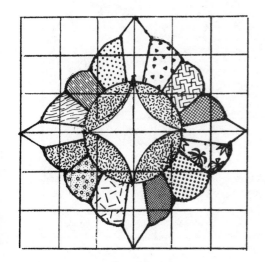

946 Fancy Dresden Plate

947 Ferris Wheel

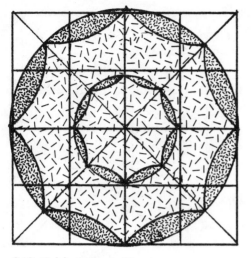

948 Odds & Ends II

949 Baseball

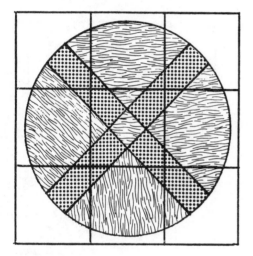

950 Circle Cross

951 Bay Leaf

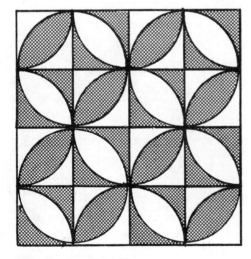

952 Orange Peel II

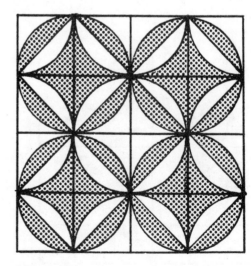

953 Robbing Peter to Pay Paul IV

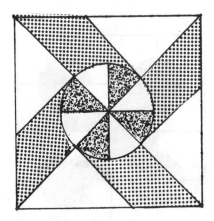

954 Boston Puzzle I

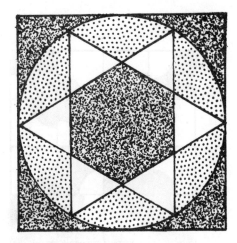

955 Savannah Star

956 Wheel of Fortune IV

957 Sun, Moon & Stars

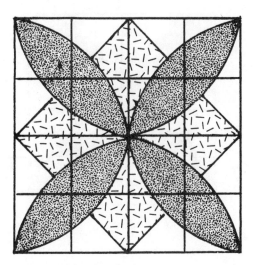

958 Tobacco Leaf

959 Trenton Quilt Block

960 Drunkard's Path

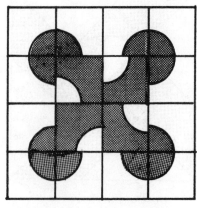

961 Wonder of the World

962 Falling Timbers

963 Vine of Friendship

964 Dove I

965 Fool's Puzzle I

966 Chain Links

967 Love Ring

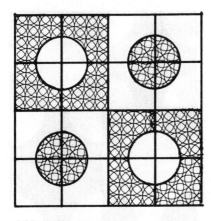

968 Polka Dot

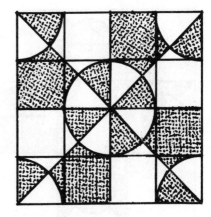

969 Snowball II

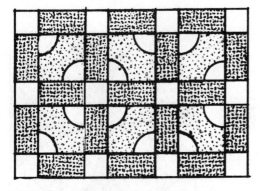

970 Grandmother's Favorite

971 Snowball III

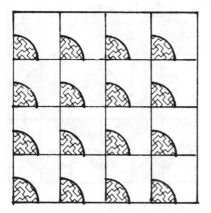

972 Unnamed

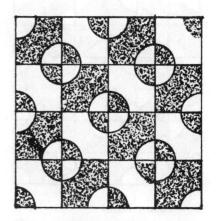

973 Steeplechase

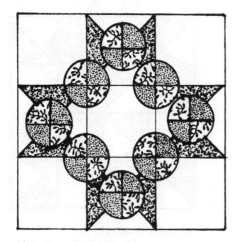

974 Snowball Wreath

975 Pullman Puzzle

976 Robbing Peter to Pay Paul V

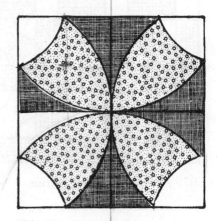

977 Winding Ways

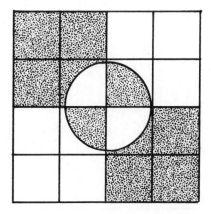

978 Robbing Peter to Pay Paul VI

979 Around the World

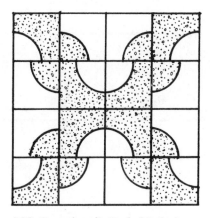

980 Drunkard's Path Variation

981 Fool's Puzzle II

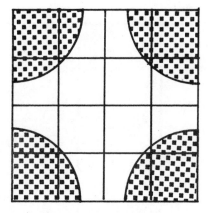

982 Millwheel II

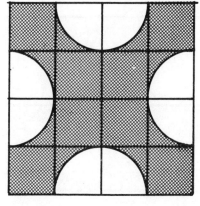

983 Boston Puzzle II

Seven-Patch Designs

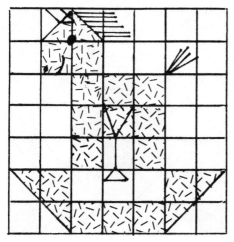

984 Hobby Horse

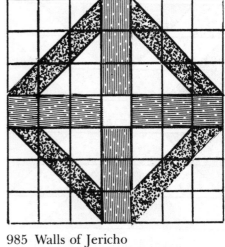

985 Walls of Jericho

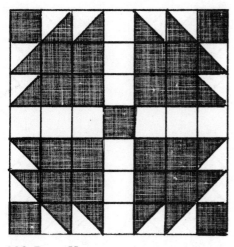

986 Dove II

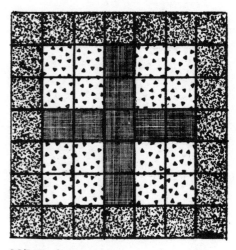

987 Red Cross VI

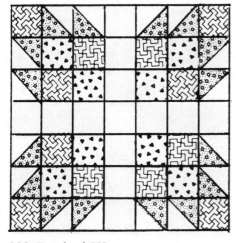

988 Rosebud III

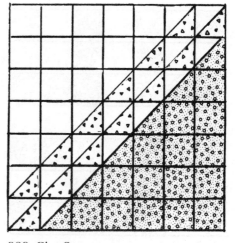

989 City Square

990 Country Roads

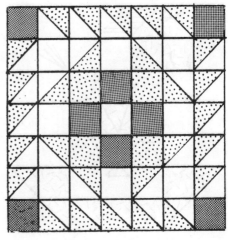

991 Prickly Pear

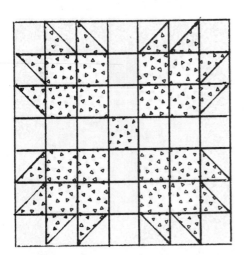

992 Bear's Paw

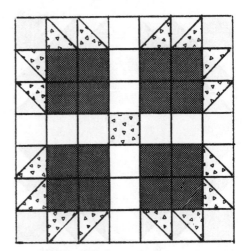

993 Bear's Tracks

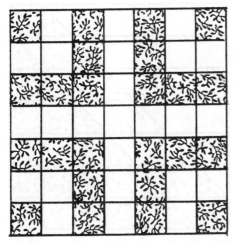

994 Stonemason's Puzzle

995 Lincoln's Platform

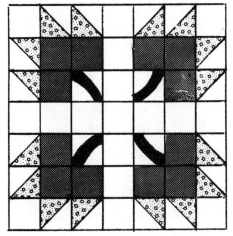

996 Autumn Leaf

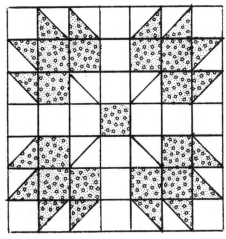

997 Peony II

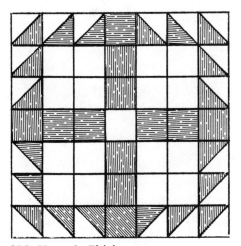

998 Hens & Chickens

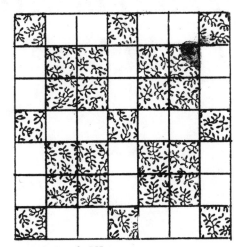

999 9-Patch VI

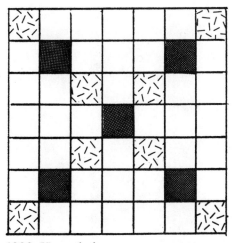

1000 Hemstitch

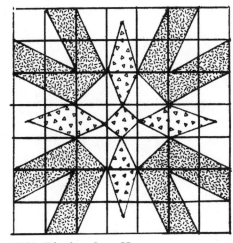

1001 Blazing Star II

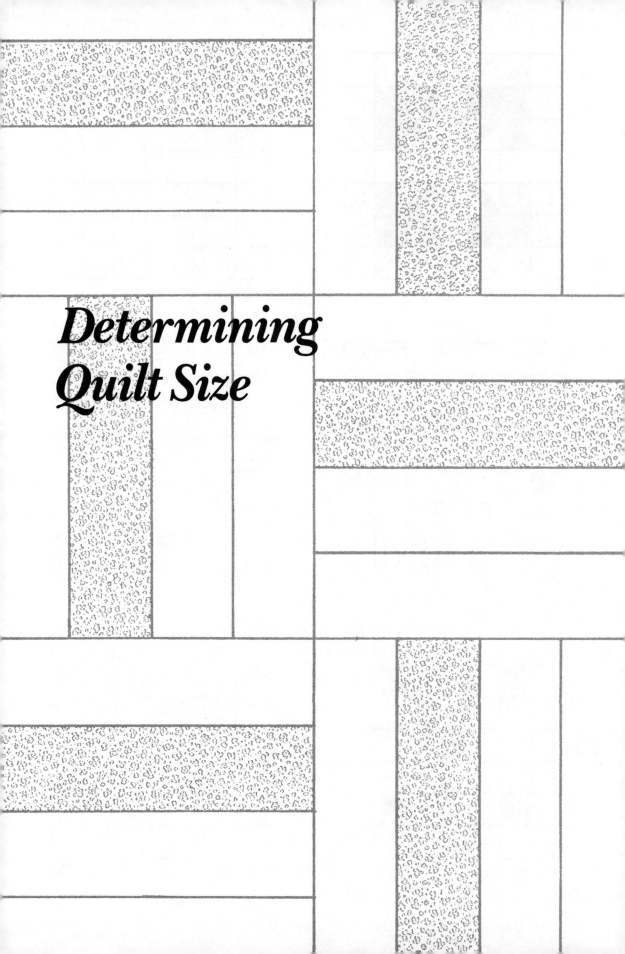

Determining Quilt Size

To determine quilt size, several factors must be taken into account. Mattress size is your first consideration. Then, do you want the quilt to fall to the floor as a bedspread, with tuck-in for the pillows, or just as a cover for the mattress? Does the style of the bed present limitations? I have an antique bed with sideboards measuring 14″ deep. I don't want the quilt to fall below the sideboards, so I am limited in the amount of overhang. A throw for the couch would be smaller, as would a baby quilt.

As a general guideline, mattress sizes are as follows:

King	72″ × 84″
Queen	60″ × 80″
Double	54″ × 75″
Twin	39″ × 75″
Cot	30″ × 75″
Crib	27″ × 50″

It's a good idea to go ahead and measure your mattress, especially if it suffers from middle-age spread. Measure from side-to-side to obtain width, and from top-to-bottom for length.

For a double-size bed, my calculations would be as follows:

Mattress size:	54″ wide × 75″ long
Allowance for pillows:	18″
Overhang at foot:	12″
Overhang on each side:	
12″ × 2 =	24″
	78″ wide × 105″ long

The next example is for a modern bed, with a double-size mattress. Mattress and box springs have a depth of 14″ and the quilt will not cover the pillows:

Mattress size:	54″ wide × 75″ long
Overhang at foot:	14″
Overhang on each side:	
14″ × 2 =	28″
	82″ wide × 89″ long

Once you've decided how large you want the quilt it's time to determine what size block you will use. You should be flexible in this area, because block size and finished quilt size usually will not come out even. The following charts illustrate the problems that arise in arriving at an approximate quilt size of 78″ × 106″:

Block Size	Blocks Across	Blocks Down	Total Blocks Needed
8″	9 = 72″ 6″ border	13 = 104″ 2″ border	117
9″	8 = 72″ 6″ border	11 = 99″ 7″ border	88
10″	7 = 70″ 8″ border	10 = 100″ 6″ border	70
12″	6 = 72″ 6″ border	8 = 96″ 10″ border	48
14″	5 = 70″ 8″ border	7 = 98″ 8″ border	35
15″	5 = 75″ 3″ border	7 = 105″ 1″ border	35

or

15″	4 = 60″ 18″ border	6 = 90″ 16″ border	24
16″	4 = 64″ 14″ border	6 = 96″ 10″ border	24
18″	4 = 72″ 6″ border	5 = 90″ 16″ border	20

As you can see, only the 14″ block size will come out evenly. If you are using a 7-patch pattern, you're in good shape and can proceed full steam ahead. However, if using any of the others, when scaling your pattern to the 14″ size, you will have to work with fractions. I avoid this at all costs and would make adjustments in the finished size.

If you decide to use a 12″ block, you can either increase the side borders to equal 10″ or cut down the end border to measure 6″. This is much simpler than working with fractions to scale the block to the 14″ size.

The above examples are for use when the patchwork is an overall design. If you wish, you can piece only the portion that will cover the mattress top and fill in the sides with borders to show off your fancy quilting stitches.

Setting the quilt with lattice strips is a very popular method. In fact, in the above examples it would be easier to set the 18″ block this way, rather than to try to adjust the borders to allow for 10″. The following chart shows the calculations and adjustments needed when using lattice strips. The quilt size is 78″ x 106″ and border and lattice strips are figured to be the same width.

Block Size	Blocks Across	Blocks Down	Total Blocks Needed
8″	8 = 64″ 9 2″ strips = 18″ Finished Size: 82″ × 102″	10 = 80″ 11 2″ strips = 22″	80
9″	7 = 63″ 8 2″ strips = 16″ Finished Size: 79″ × 101″	9 = 81″ 10 2″ strips = 20″	63
10″	6 = 60″ 7 3″ strips = 21″ Finished Size: 81″ × 107″	8 = 80″ 9 3″ strips = 27″	48
12″	5 = 60″ 6 3″ strips = 18″ Finished Size: 78″ × 108″	7 = 84″ 8 3″ strips = 24″	35
14″	4 = 56″ 5 3″ strips = 15″ Finished Size: 71″ × 105″ (This size may be better if set solid.)	6 = 84″ 7 3″ strips = 21″	24
15″	4 = 60″ 5 3″ strips = 15″ Finished Size: 75″ × 94″ *If the lattice strips are made 4″ wide:* 5 4″ strips = 20″ Finished Size: 80″ × 99″	5 = 75″ 6 3″ strips = 18″ 6 4″ strips = 24″	20
16″	4 = 64″ 5 4″ strips = 20″ Finished Size: 84″ × 104″	5 = 80″ 6 4″ strips = 24″	20
18″	3 = 54″ 4 4″ strips = 16″ Finished Size: 70″ × 92″	4 = 72″ 5 4″ strips = 20″	

The lattice strips could be increased to 5″ or 6″ in width.

Blocks set on the diagonal must be multiplied by 1.42 to determine the finished size of the quilt. The following shows the width of the blocks and rounds it off to the nearest $\frac{1}{2}$.

8″ block = 11.36 or 11½″
9″ block = 12.78 or 13″
10″ block = 14.2 or 14″
11″ block = 15.62 or 15½″
12″ block = 17.04 or 17″
13″ block = 18.46 or 18½″
14″ block = 19.88 or 20″
15″ block = 21.3 or 21½″
16″ block = 22.72 or 22½″
17″ block = 24.14 or 24″
18″ block = 25.56 or 25½″

The foregoing may seem like a lot of unnecessary math, but some familiarity with it will be helpful to you. Before you can figure the amount of fabric to buy, you must know how many blocks you need to complete the top. For a double bed, you can get some idea just by using the figures given here. Even if you have to figure it out, you'll only have to do it once since you're making quilts for the same size bed most of the time. I almost always use a 12″ block, the quilt set solid with no border, so I automatically know I need 48 blocks.

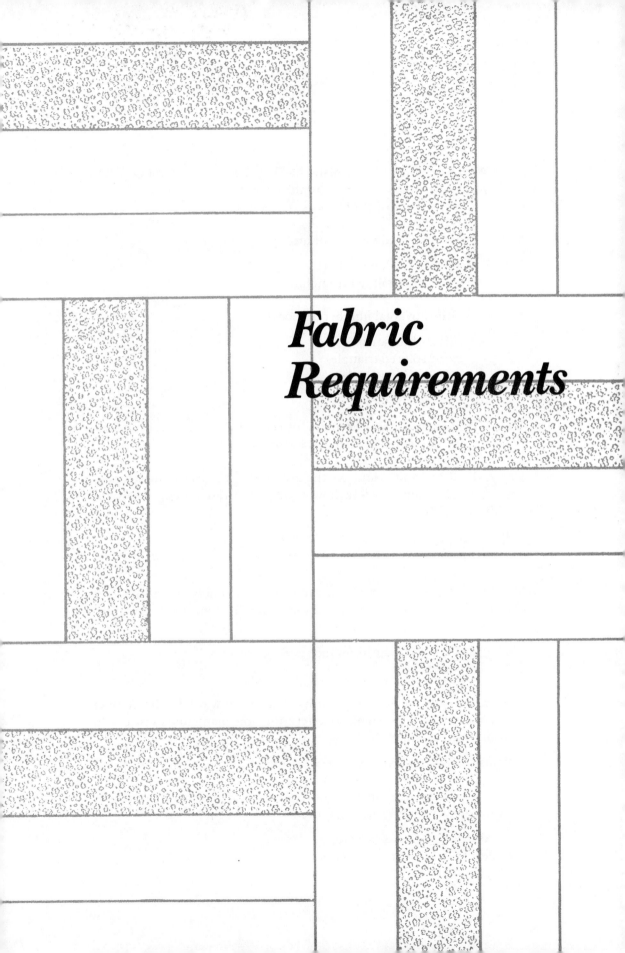

Fabric Requirements

Once you have determined how many blocks are needed for the quilt top you are ready to estimate how much fabric you need. I'll use the Friendship Star, p. 000, scaled to a 12″ block as an example.

Step 1: Determine total number of units per block.

4 white squares, 1 colored square
4 white triangles, 4 colored triangles

Step 2: Multiply by total number of blocks.

$4 \times 48 = 192$ white squares
192 colored triangles
192 white triangles
48 colored squares

Step 3: Add seam allowances to one of each of the units needed. Measure width and length of each of these units.

Step 4: Find the unit width on the accompanying chart. Go across to the second column to find how many units can be cut across the width of the fabric.

4″ square plus ½″ seam allowance = 5″ square
9 units across fabric

Step 5: Find the unit length on the chart and follow it across to the third column to see how many units can be cut from the length of the fabric.

4″ square plus ½″ seam allowance = 5″ square
7 units down fabric

Step 6: Multiply the number of units obtained in width by the number of units obtained in length to determine how many units can be cut from 1 yard of fabric.

9 units across $\times$ 7 units down = 63 per yard

Step 7: Divide total number of units needed by number of units per yard to obtain total yardage required.

192 divided by 63 = 3.04 yards
Repeat for each unit of block.

Unit Size	Number of Units Across (45" fabric)	Number of Units Down (36" fabric)
1"	45	36
1½"	30	24
2"	22	18
2½"	18	14
3"	15	12
3½"	12	10
4"	11	9
4½"	10	8
5"	9	7
5½"	8	6
6"	7	6
6½"	6	5
7"	6	5
7½"	6	4
8"	5	4
8½"	5	4
9"	4	4

Quilting

Quilting is the finishing touch to your patchwork top. The main purpose of the quilting stitches is to hold the three layers of the quilt together, but it has evolved into a highly decorative design element. In fact, many excellent examples of tops that were quilted only are in museums around the country. For many, this is the most enjoyable part of making the quilt.

As I've already mentioned, I like designing the tops, and don't get that involved with the actual quilting. I do it all on the machine to get it over with. Surprisingly, even intricate feather patterns can be executed on the sewing machine, if you've taken the time to learn what your machine can do.

Fillers or Batts

The filler is the material that goes in the middle, between the top and the lining.

Cotton batts. A cotton material in batt form. It must be closely quilted, with no more than an inch between the quilting lines because the batt will shift and bunch up when washed. It gives a rather flat appearance to the finished quilting.

Bonded polyester batts. This is a polyester material which has been treated to hold the fibres together. It is easy to work with since the layers of the batt will not shred or tear, giving a smooth uniform surface. The finished quilt has a higher loft and the quilting stitches stand out in relief. It need not be quilted as closely as cotton batts; two to four inches is usually sufficient.

Unbonded batts. These batts give a very soft, fluffy appearance to the finished quilt. Like the bonded batts, they are easy to work with during the sewing step, but care must be taken when spreading the batt on the top since it will shred, leaving thick and thin spots. You will have to pull off pieces from the thick spots or along the edges to fill in the thin spots. It, too, can be quilted two to four inches apart.

Lining or Backing Fabrics

Your choice is unlimited as to what you use to back your quilt with; yard goods, sheets, flannel or lightweight blankets are all suitable. You can still occasionally pick up fabrics for under a dollar a yard when the fabric stores have sales. Sheets are frequently on sale at very reasonable prices and can be used both for the backing and as material for the top. If you're near an outlet store, fabrics can be purchased for about half of what you would pay at your ordinary retail store. And don't overlook flea markets and rummage sales. You won't often find good fabrics here, but now and then you may hit a bonanza.

Assembling the Quilt

Lay the top wrong-side-up on a large, flat surface. Spread the batting over the top and smooth it out.

Seam the backing fabric together to the width of the quilt top, plus 1" or 2" all around. This extra allowance is especially important when doing machine quilting. This extra margin of fabric allows for any shifting of the fabric as you sew.

Whole-top Quilting

Step one is to loosen the pressure on the presser foot. This helps cut down on the shifting and pushing of the fabric, which is the major problem in machine quilting.

Do not baste the layers of the quilt together. I place several large pins around the edges of the quilt to help hold it while I begin sewing. If you baste, the fabric tends to pile up on the basting stitches causing puckers and ripples. By cutting the backing fabric slightly larger, I can smooth the fabric in front of the presser foot, taking out all wrinkles as I sew.

A large table on which to sew is an absolute must. It helps keep the quilt flat, cutting down on the amount of shifting you will experience. Position your sewing machine at one end of the table so you can spread the quilt out.

Slide the edge of the quilt under the presser foot and roll it up to the center. The center section is the most difficult because so much fabric is rolled under the machine. As you move out towards the edges, it gets easier. Following the seam line from the center, stitch to the outer edge of the quilt, smoothing out the fabric as you go. Do two or three rows in this direction, then turn the quilt and go in the opposite direction. This alternating technique helps keep the quilt smooth and flat.

If your top is of a simple design that requires only straight-line stitching, you can start at one end of the quilt and work to the other end. In this case, the backing fabric should be longer on the end toward which you are sewing so that any shift in the fabric is covered by the backing when finished. Always start sewing at the same end.

By the Block

This is an easy way to quilt, either by hand or machine, because you are working with only one block at a time. For intricate designs this method is by far the best, since the block is easy to manipulate under the needle.

Cut the filler the size of the finished block, and the backing one inch larger than the block. Lay the three layers together and quilt in the design, being sure that you do not quilt beyond the seam line into the seam allowance.

To assemble the blocks. Turn back the seam allowance on the backing and push the filler out of the way. Lay the quilted blocks right sides together and stitch the seams, being sure you do not catch in the backing or filler. Continue adding blocks until the first row is complete, then repeat for each succeeding row. Join the rows in the same manner.

Finishing the back. Smooth the batting down and trim off any excess. It should meet in the middle of the seam. Smooth one side of the backing down. Turn under the seam allowance on the other seam and lay over the first one. Stitch with a slipstitch.

A really nice finish for the back is to place lattice strips over the seams and stitch in place.

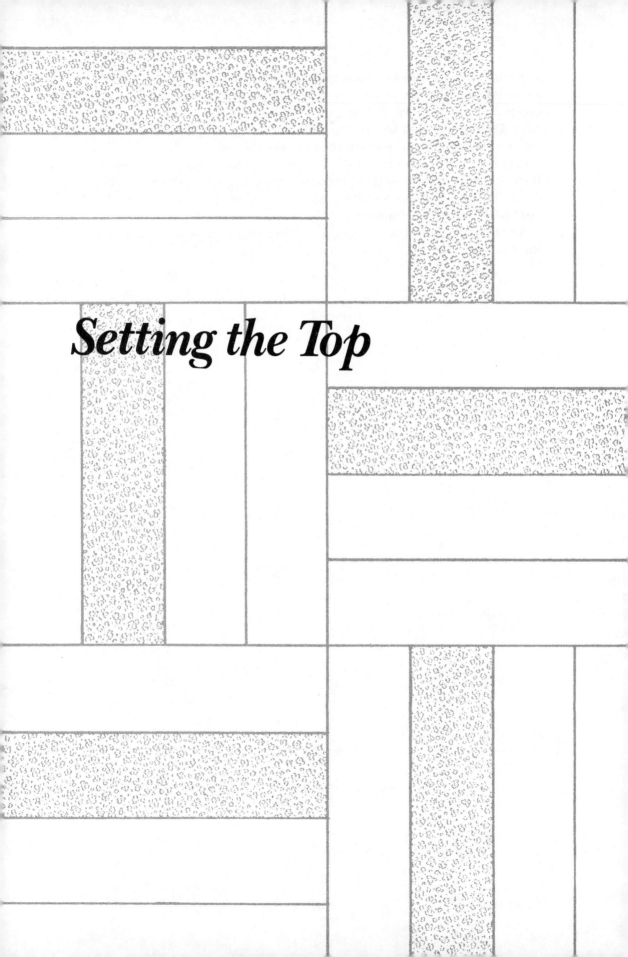

Setting the Top

The final step in assembling the quilt top is the setting. I find this to be the most exciting part of the entire quiltmaking process. Using the Ohio Star pattern, I've illustrated five different ways you can set the top, thereby giving you five different quilts.

The simplest method is to alternate plain and pieced blocks. With this setting you only have to piece half as many blocks, and it also provides more space for decorative quilting.

One of the most popular methods is to set the blocks solid. This setting gives an overall design, but many times you will be surprised. Secondary designs stand out only after the blocks have been assembled. The Wind-blown Square pattern is designed to be set with alternate white blocks, but I decided to set it solid. As illustrated, the basic design is lost and a pattern of pinwheels emerges.

The use of lattice strips to separate the blocks is another popular setting method, especially if the pattern has been executed in scrap fabrics. The lattice strips pull the design together into a coherent whole. And again, you don't need to piece as many blocks because the lattice strips add to the size of the quilt with little additional work.

Many blocks are designed to be set on the diagonal, but you should also try setting some of your favorite patterns diagonally. You may be pleasantly surprised by a stunning new quilt pattern.

Lattice strips are also effective on a diagonally set quilt. They can either blend in by being the same color as the background blocks or you can set the design off by using color in the strips. The long lines of solid color enhance and accentuate a diagonal design.

Color is the only important thing to consider when designing a quilt top. Color creates the design and whatever impact each design element has. It creates the tone and mood of the quilt. A design executed in browns, beiges and oranges will have a masculine feel, while the same design executed in pastels will be feminine in mood.

If you're new to quilting, don't let color frighten you. You can start by using the colors suggested in the pattern you're making. Or use colors that you like and use every day. When you shop for fabric, lay different colors together, then stand back and see what the effect of the combination is. Keep in mind that from a distance the design of the fabric doesn't show, only the color.

It's fun to experiment. All you need is some graph paper and colored markers. Draw the design on the graph paper and try out your ideas. If you have several you want to try, it would probably be easier to have some photocopies run of the design, so that you don't have to keep drawing it over and over.

The two Ohio Star variations came about using this method. The blue design is merely a change in color placement. The second one is achieved in the same manner, but the overall design doesn't come out until four blocks are set together. Lattice strips join each four-block unit.

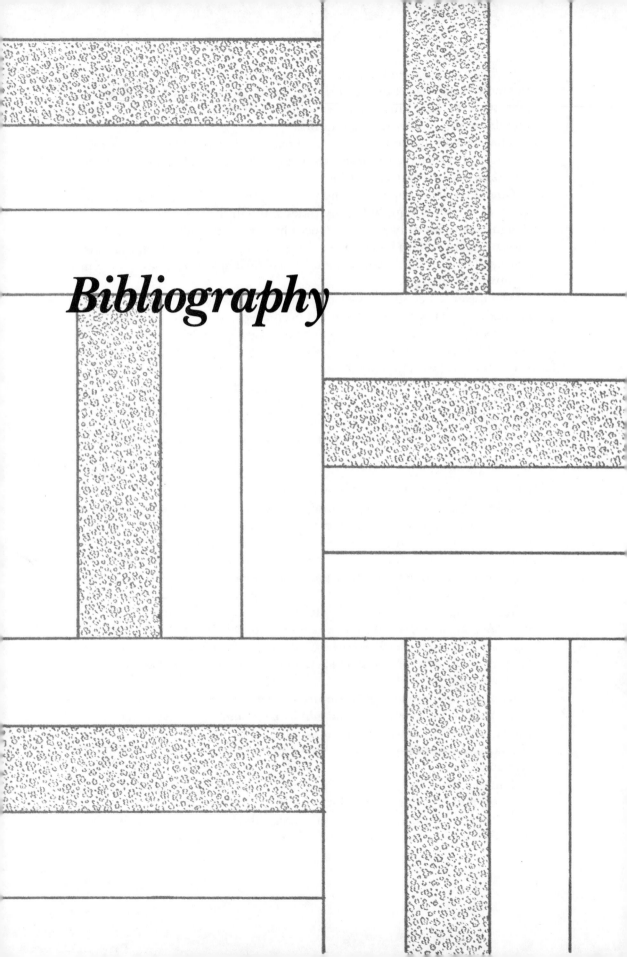

Bibliography

Bishop, Robert, *New Discoveries in American Quilts*. New York: E. P. Dutton & Company, 1975

Gutcheon, Beth, *The Perfect Patchwork Primer*. New York: Penguin Books, 1974

Hall, Carrie A. and Kretsinger, Rose G., *The Romance of the Patchwork Quilt in America*. New York: Bonanza Books, 1935

Hechtlinger, Adelaide, *American Quilts, Quilting and Patchwork*. Harrisburg, Pa.: Stackpole Books, 1974

Hinson, Dorothy A., *A Quilter's Companion*. New York: Arco Publishing Company, 1973

Holstein, Jonathan, *The Pieced Quilt, and American Design Tradition*. New York: New York Graphic Society, 1975

Ickis, Marguerite, *The Standard Book of Quilt Making and Collecting*. New York: Dover Publications, 1949

Khin, Yvonne M., *The Collectors Dictionary of Quilt Names and Patterns*. Washington, D.C.: Acropolis Books, 1980

Lithgow, Marilyn, *Quiltmaking & Quiltmakers*. New York: Funk & Wagnalls, 1974

Malone, Maggie, *Classic American Patchwork Quilt Patterns*. New York: Sterling Publishing Company, 1979

McKim, Ruby, *One Hundred & One Patchwork Patterns*. New York: Dover Publications, 1962

Pforr, Effie Chalmers, *Award Winning Quilts*. Birmingham, Ala.: Oxmoor House, Inc., 1974

Risinger, Hettie, *Innovative Machine Quilting*. New York: Sterling Publishing Company, 1980

Safford, Carleton L. and Bishop, Robert, *America's Quilts and Coverlets*. Barre, Mass.: Weathervane Books, 1974

PERIODICALS

Quilt World, House of White Birches
Quilt, Harris Publications
Ladies Circle Patchwork Quilts
Quilter's Newsletter, Leman Publications

Index

INDEX

Number enclosed in parentheses is the number of the design. The second number is the page number.